Those Preachin' Women

SERMONS BY BLACK WOMEN PREACHERS

Ella Pearson Mitchell, editor

Judson Press® Valley Forge

THOSE PREACHIN' WOMEN

Library of Congress Cataloging in Publication Data
Main entry under title:

Those preachin' women.

    1. Sermons, American. 2. Women clergy.
I. Mitchell, Ella Pearson.
BV4241.T475   1985   252   85-4731
ISBN 0-8170-1073-4

10 09 08 07 06 05 04 03 02
16 15 14 13 12 11 10 9 8 7
Printed in the U.S.A.

*This effort is dedicated to
all the mothers of
all the authors.*

———————

———————

————————————

Contents

Foreword

The subject of women in ministry in Christian churches has long been an issue of controversy. Indeed, there have been times when the debate has become so heated that in its name the relations of Christians, congregations, and even denominations have been fractured. It may be that in the present hour God is resolving the debate and setting aside the controversy, for it is an incontestable fact that the living Lord is choosing to lay claim upon the lives of an ever-increasing number of women and charging them to preach the gospel of Jesus Christ. And daily women are answering yes to that all-compelling call of God.

The response of these twentieth-century messengers is not without precedent. Although the tradition in which they stand has often been obscured by prejudice, it is, nevertheless, as old as Christian discipleship. Repeatedly, in defiance of the patriarchal exclusions of first-century culture, our Lord prepared women for ministry. Jesus welcomed women into his itinerant seminary, held high-level theological discussion about the nature of God and the character of true worship with a Samaritan woman at Jacob's well, commended Mary of Bethany for choosing to learn the truths of God at his feet, and transformed women mourners into women messengers at the site of the empty tomb. Commissioned by none other than the risen Christ, women first proclaimed the resurrection. Two thousand years later their daughters announce to disciples and to doubters, "We have seen the Lord."

The sermons that follow are offered in obedience to that commission. The proclaimers are unapologetically Black women preachers. Their identity is grounded in the intrinsic dynamic of each of these realities. Their messages are forged in the crucible of their experience of blackness, femaleness, and the liberation of God in Jesus Christ. Their response to the call of God has often been the product of protracted struggle. Yet when the "yes" finally ushered from the center of their being, they knew that it had been there all the time and that before they were even formed in the womb they were called and anointed. Like Jeremiah they learned that to refuse to preach is to experience a fire in one's bones that can be quenched by nothing less than faithful, obedient preaching.

Those of us who in the present hour seek to undertake this awful and wondrous assignment are grateful to God for the Reverend Ella Pearson Mitchell—daughter of God, mother in the gospel ministry, role model, teacher, and friend. This volume is the fruit of her loving labor. For it and for the ministries of the preachers who share in it, we give God thanks.

Let us read that we might hear, and hear that we might heal.

Prathia Hall Wynn
Philadelphia, Pennsylvania

Introduction

Women in the Ministry

The hour has come. As a daughter of God I feel the weight of the mantle, and so I must proclaim the message as best I can—"A Woman's Word from the Lord" from a primarily biblical perspective.

I am convinced that women were ordained to be in ministry from the very beginning of time. However, the biblical record is not entirely unequivocal on the subject, especially for surface readers bent on selecting proof texts that presumably support their position of advantage. Nevertheless the *Christian* church was launched on a platform of nondiscrimination against women, and everybody knows that when the Holy Ghost came at Pentecost, Peter's very sermon declared: "And it shall come to pass in the last days, saith God, I will pour out of my spirit upon all flesh: and your sons and your daughters shall prophesy . . ." (Acts 2:17).

The text was good enough for Peter, who was not notably liberal or "far out" but, rather, was a *very conservative* preacher, to say the least. Peter was first under obligation to explain that the strange behavior manifested in the upper room was spiritual ecstasy and not intoxication. Then he proceeded to reach back to the prophet Joel to say that this was, *in fact*, what God promised would happen. Now at Pentecost God was doing it: pouring out the Spirit on *all* flesh. The revelation was not admonishing male exclusivism, per se, but declaring the generous outpouring of the Holy Spirit, after which both sons and daughters would prophesy.

The very first and foundational proclamation from the text is that God pours out his spirit indiscriminately. *That* flesh, thereafter, is commissioned to bear the message as Jesus had proclaimed in Acts 1:8: "But ye shall receive power, after that the Holy Ghost is come upon you: and ye shall be witnesses unto me both in Jerusalem, and in all Judea, and in Samaria, and unto the uttermost part of the earth."

The first facet of the text has long been popular and valid in liberation dimensions. God has, for sure, been known by Black folks to be no respecter of persons, classes, or races. Therefore, we rejoice in knowing that whatever areas of discriminations are promoted by us humans, God ultimately intends to deal with all of us without distinction. It remains only for those of us who have long enjoyed this powerful biblical affirmation to apply it also to different genders. *All* flesh will brook no less a universality of application. If you are wondering how I can so quickly insist that this "gender distinction" is not biblical, let me suggest that it is not in the Word—the Word has no limitations or specifications on the *all flesh*. But I can also say that in this world, in this life, I have seen fantastic concrete evidence of this same thing. Indeed, it's been going on in the Black church for a long, long time. At the very beginning of the Black church in America near the end of the eighteenth century, there was a woman named Jarena Lee. Bishop Richard Allen freely admitted that she was a very gifted preacher. In fact, on one occasion when a conference preacher turned out to be totally unequal to the hour of power, Jarena rose up and took his text and proclaimed, "Thus saith the Lord," with clarity and relevance seldom heard in those circles. Bishop Allen admitted that surely she had been called of God to preach. Yet, even in the face of the fact that God's power and spirit had been poured out on her, Allen used the rules of the White Methodist church from which he had withdrawn to deter her ordination. She was never assigned a church or even given any clergy status. But she *was* a preacher.

In the seminaries I see a contemporary parallel of God's gifts to women as class after class of graduates is led by one of its small number of women. The spirit poured forth to bless two daughters of God to be the first and second place graduates at one seminary, and both of them were over forty years of age. Indeed, it was this kind of example that eventually broke me away from my old conformity to the restrictions placed on women. I never wanted to admit I was preaching, but time after time when I spoke, miracles would take place; God did bless.

I remember one Sunday when a licensed preacher presiding from the lofty pulpit ordered me to speak from the floor of the sanctuary and decreed that he would extend the invitation. When I had finished speaking from the text "We have these treasures in earthen vessels," he sensed that it would be utter nonsense for him to intervene. He signaled for me to open the doors of the church, which I did. The response to that invitation still brings a warm affirmation to my ministry, for *four* adult men and one young woman came forward—three of the men and the woman as candidates for baptism and the fourth man coming by Christian experience. One of the men had been a Catholic all of his life.

I shall never forget how, on another Sunday in a remodeled garage in a California city, eleven souls came forward to surrender their lives to Christ. This time nine of them were candidates for baptism. The pastor, God bless him, with tears in his eyes proclaimed things about my ministry that up to that time I had not had the nerve even to *think* for myself. God moves in mysterious and unrestricted ways. God said that he would pour out his Spirit on all flesh, and he has dumped the bucket on a whole lot of women a whole lot of times. He poured it out on me many times before I rose up and came forward, before I made it known that as far back as my teen years I had been called by God, called to *preach* as well as to *teach*. This is in the mind and will of God, and God who changeth not has never willed it otherwise. It's we faltering humans who have the hangups.

God has been trying all the time to break through the cultural bias that has prevailed. Women have been "put down" almost universally, perhaps because males of the species have stronger muscles and more commanding voices. It has been, as we Blacks know so well, a game of power. And in that game women of all ages have had the disadvantage of less physical power. And so they were written into the culture at a subordinate position. Even here, however, one sees blinding shafts of light indicating that God is breaking through those cultural biases and progressively revealing himself in ever higher dimensions in regard to women—just as God has done in regard to minorities.

Certainly one of the most dramatic instances of God's breakthrough is to be seen in the story of Deborah, found in the fourth chapter of the Book of Judges. This woman is most often remembered as a Joan-of-Arc type, leading a victorious army of God's people after their own general refused to go to war without her. But her spiritual significance far outweighs the heroic acts mentioned. Deborah rose from keeper of the lamps to counselor to the people to great judge in Israel, a position at the very apex of both church and state authority. Deborah was used of God to revive and revitalize God's people as no man in her time was apparently able to do. God broke through in a most impressive way with Deborah.

Let me invite your attention to one more such breakthrough that seemed to have been God's will. In both 2 Kings 22:12-20 and 2 Chronicles 34:19-28, there are accounts of the crucial contribution of a prophet named Huldah. The incident occurred after the scrolls of the law were found by the builders working on the restoration of the temple.

> And it came to pass, when the king had heard the words of the law, that he rent his clothes. And the king commanded Hilkiah, and Ahikam . . . and Asaiah servant of the kings, saying, Go,

inquire of the LORD for me. . . . And Hilkiah, and they that the king had appointed, went to Huldah the prophetess, the wife of Shallum the son of Tikvath, the son of Hasrah, keeper of the wardrobe; (now she dwelt . . . in the college). . . . She answered them, Thus saith the LORD God of Israel . . . (2 Chronicles 34:19-23).

Note that the writer forgot to have Josiah mention the name of the woman he sent his elite to consult, even though Josiah was very young and no doubt accustomed to consulting women such as his mother. The only fact stated about Huldah was that she lived in the second quarter, the newer part, of Jerusalem. All else pertained to her husband, whose family tree was presented and whose family had positions as keepers of the king's wardrobe. We have no notion of who Huldah's father and mother were, and we know nothing else about her save the fact that she was so highly respected that King Josiah *and* the high priests dared not move on their findings without her judgment. They had to believe what the Holy Spirit would reveal to her in a way not common among them. We can sense how they must have felt. Her prophecy, the first by a woman, was one of the few fulfilled in detail.

I cite all of this simply to suggest that God, again, was trying to break through the cultural bias by means of the choice of vessels for the Holy Spirit. Despite the fact that later historians did not share Josiah's opinion of Huldah, his feelings of great respect break through. Inspired though they must have been, the historians were creatures of their culture, and God had to transcend that culture by a major act.

Much later in the Old Testament, after the Exile and perhaps around the year 345 B.C., God broke through again by means of the mouth of the eloquent prophet Joel. When he spoke of the powerful call to repentance, Joel prophesied that God would pour out His spirit on *all* flesh.

> "And it shall come to pass afterward,
>   that I will pour out my spirit on all flesh;
> your sons and daughters shall prophesy;
>   your old men shall dream dreams,
>   and your young men shall see visions.
> Even upon the menservants and maidser-
> vants

in those days, I will pour out my spirit."
—Joel 2:28-29 (RSV)

It was this text that Peter quoted again in his long and historic sermon on the day of Pentecost. God broke through that day when the people all heard it or didn't hear it. God laid down his fundamental principle *and* will. Previous Old Testament prophets had talked of God's promise to Israel, but here was Joel saying God's blessings would be on *all* flesh, regardless of nationality, race, age, sex, or social rank.

In the New Testament we read of another marvelous breakthrough, embodied in a woman named Priscilla. She and her husband were tentmakers. No doubt the apostle Paul spent long hours with them, not only earning a living but also teaching the Christian faith. The day came when these two dedicated persons heard a preacher named Apollos — a man of great talent and impact. Apollos had been born in Alexandria and was an eloquent proclaimer of Old Testament Scriptures, as Acts 18:24 indicates. He was quite fervent in the spirit and taught diligently, but he knew only of the baptism of John. It was in the synagogue that Priscilla and Aquilla heard Apollos preach. They took him unto themselves and they expounded to Apollos more perfectly, concerning the *words of the Lord*. Acts 18:26 says that the most eloquent preacher of the early church was taught by Prisca— taught by the woman who was probably Paul's best theological student. It might be uncomfortable for some of us to study with female professors, but God does use women as teachers of male preachers.

To be sure, the question arises as to how on earth this Paul, who was presumably quoted in Timothy as telling women to "shut up," should have been so comfortable knowing that his chief competitor, Apollos, was indirectly instructed by *him* through the theologian and scholar, Priscilla. Wait—this was not the only time Paul obviously took for granted the ministry of women. In 1 Corinthians 11:5 Paul casually wrote that women who were praying and prophesying in public should follow the conservative Jewish custom, nevertheless, and should cover their heads. He also showed the same position with his apparent acceptance of Philip's four daughters, all of whom prophesied, as mentioned in Acts 21:8-9. In other words, when we read Paul in 1 Corinthians 14:34, "Let your women keep silence in the church," we have to look at the larger context, using the light of the totality of Paul's writings to get any real sense of what that instruction is all about. Everything that is written is not of the same level of inspiration, and Paul provides some good examples of this. At several points he said things like "I say this by permission and not by commandment." In so doing, he clearly established both the fact that he was aware of his own personal bias about women and the fact that he knew God didn't reveal such a bias. He is, in other words, a clear example of the principle that God keeps breaking through. In Galatians 3 one hears Paul make no qualifications: "For ye are all the children of God by faith in Christ Jesus. . . . There is neither Jew nor Greek, there is neither bond nor free, there is neither male nor female: for ye are *all* one in Christ Jesus (Galatians 3:26-28, emphasis added).

I suppose one can meet Paul at his workaday best, however, in Ephesians 5 and 6. Here Paul was engaged in a kind of pastoral attack that helps us to understand where Paul's head was on a number of controversial issues. Indeed, Paul shows us how we may do a better job of leading people into new ideas. He was concerned about the treatment of children, women, and slaves—all of whom we recognize as powerless people. And in each case Paul's comments start with phrases that gained the ears of his audience by solidly affirming what those in power most wanted to hear. He said, "Children, obey your parents," and having thus established attention and interest, he moved to the new breakthrough principle: even though children are powerless, "Parents, provoke not your children to wrath." He said to wives, "Obey; submit to your husbands," and then he came to the breakthrough principle; "But husbands, love your wives and give yourselves for them completely, even as Christ gave himself for the church." He continued on, saying to the slaves, "Slaves obey your masters." After getting the masters' ears, he said what most defenders of slavery leave out or forget: "Remember, masters, you slothful rascals, there is but one Master and that is *God*."

Now for those who want women to be subordinate and who wish to quote Paul, let me warn you that if you take Paul's introductory statement rather than his breakthrough, you must do the same thing for slaves. And in that case, you would have to be a slave and find yourself a master. As we look at all this, we have to see that what Paul said about women being forbidden to usurp authority over men does not mean what it seems to say, and it never *could* if you read *all* of the Bible.

Let us reflect for a moment more on the whole notion of God as a breakthrough revelator. At times in theological circles we have referred to this idea as a kind of progressive revelation. One sees this in the words of Jesus himself when he told the story known as the parable of the cruel vine-dressers. It is found in Matthew 21:33-41; Mark 12:1-9; and Luke 20:1-16. In all three accounts, God kept sending servants who were not heard or permitted to work; indeed, they were badly abused and almost destroyed. Finally, when he sent his beloved son, the vinedressers cast him out of the vineyard and killed him. God kept trying to break through, and Jesus himself was the zenith in this series of God's breakthrough revelations.

The breakthroughs most often start at points that we are not comfortable looking at. They go all the way back to early Hebrew history. We see Abraham caught in a culture that believed in the sacrifice of children. God breaks through and says to Abraham, "I'm glad you're willing to show me how much you trust me with your beloved son, but STOP! STOP! I'm breaking through and stopping this thing right here and now!" Now look with me at Deuteronomy 21:18-21, where the law sounds terrible but where God is breaking through, even so. The account says that when a child was an incorrigible delinquent, parents should take him to the gate where the elders sit, prefer charges against him, and when the elders have judged him, stone the poor child to death. That sounds abusive and terrible; nevertheless, it is a breakthrough, for prior to that time fathers could kill irreclaimable sons outright and even mothers could not intervene. When we study this passage, we become aware of the wife's involvement, which is a significant breakthrough. Furthermore, it appears that the child has a right to fair trial, also a breakthrough. The use of capital punishment remains to be wiped out in a later breakthrough. It is too bad that God has to continue breaking through, but, you see, we all are imperfect and resistant.

But let me tell you that God will not use patient methods to break through forever! Just as our foreparents did not have to worry about whether the masters would respond to break-through revelations against the system, so women, too, can trust the eschatological fulfillment of God's will. Joel was a certified prophet, and he prophesied what God was going to do. He said that in those last days God was going to have things his way—God would pour out his spirit on *all* flesh! God has never been a respecter of persons. We are God's children created in his image, and God's will has not changed. This is not just wishful thinking. This is the prophetic *word* of God. This will be! Prophecy has always been for right and righteousness. Prophecy has always suggested the ultimate triumph of God.

Our foreparents rejoiced in this and engaged in something we theologians call "realized eschatology." They sang about judgment day—"In that great gettin' up morning, fare you well." Oh, how they celebrated judgment day, "right now!" And they enjoyed it because they *knew* God was going to set them free.

Today, we of that oppressed body known as women, the female of the species, still believe that God has prophesied our liberation; God has declared *what* he will do *in* us and *with* us, and we know that liberation will come to pass. It may be evidenced by a number of means, in a number of ways, but it will come. I would hate to see it come to pass by a mass revolution, and I don't suspect it ever will. Although we women are in the numerical and financial majority in our churches, a great many of us, like some of the slaves, love our chains and shackles too well to change.

The liberation of women could come to pass by a kind of selective patronage, such as the prophets of Opportunities Industrialization Centers (OIC) did in Philadelphia in the sixties. My hope is that it will come to pass in the church, not because people stop paying preachers who will not accept women in the ministry, but rather because preachers who prophesy the will of God will see the church as a liberated family in which *everybody* is *used* of God! Such ministers will see the church strengthened by the intelligence and insight and, indeed, by the graciousness of women, which we call grace, and that for the salvation of all the world—all flesh!

There is a sense, you see, in which the fulfillment of God's will for women, for men, and for all the church is a means of bringing to the church a whole new dimension of theology and *grace* and, ultimately, *hope*!

That day is not to be feared. It is to be a day of rejoicing, "in that great gettin' up morning. . . ." This is a way of saying that's the way it should be—that's the way it's supposed to be *now*! And as we celebrate the coming of the will of God, we can rejoice that the day is already here.

"And he shall reign forever and ever," for he reigns even now. Hallelujah! Hallelujah! Praise the Lord Our God!

Ella Pearson Mitchell

Can Your Bones Live?

Laura Lee Sinclair

Ezekiel 37:14

One day about fifteen years ago, I brought home from work a plant that looked as though it were dead. It had only a stem, no leaves. I gave it to my husband, who has a green thumb, and I asked him, "Can this plant live?" He looked at the plant and said yes; then he began to nurture the plant. The plant still lives today, and we have been able to share that plant with many people.

Our Scripture today reminds me of my plant. Ezekiel was in a valley that had nothing but dry bones all around. An arm here, a leg there, just dry bones everywhere. God looked at these bones and asked Ezekiel, "Can these bones live?"

Dr. Laura Lee Sinclair is an ordained American Baptist minister on staff as the assistant pastor of the Antioch Baptist Church, Corona, New York. She earned her M.Div. at Union Theological Seminary of New York City, and her D.Min. at Hartford Seminary, Connecticut. She is the dean of the Antioch Bible Institute and adjunct professor at New Brunswick Theological Seminary and Lehman College. She is active in community affairs and a mentor for American Baptist Women in Ministry.

Now I'm sure that Ezekiel wanted to say no, for he knew how these bones became dry. He knew that their dryness was an indictment on Israel for specific sins that the nation had committed. These sins included cultic abuse, such as profaning of the sabbath, and ethical crimes, such as bloodshed, adultery, extortion, dishonor of parents, and the violation of the rights of orphans, widows, and sojourners. But Ezekiel also knew that the God he served was merciful and compassionate and that anything was possible with God. So he said, "O Lord, thou knowest." And sure enough, the mercy and compassion of God came forth. God told Ezekiel to preach to the bones, to tell them to hear the word of the Lord, and he, God, would cause them to live.

Ezekiel was obedient to God, and he preached to the bones. He saw something happen that I am sure astounded him. Many times the Lord will give his servant a directive, and the servant will look at it and say, "I'll do it, but I know that it will only be an exercise because I know that nothing will happen."

Well, to Ezekiel's surprise, as he preached, he heard noise and saw the bones shaking; he saw them coming together. He saw toe bones connected to foot bones, foot bones connected to ankle bones, ankle bones connected to leg bones, leg bones connected to knee bones, knee bones connected to thigh bones, thigh bones connected to hip bones, hip bones connected to back bones, back bones connected to chest bones, chest bones connected to shoulder bones, shoulder bones connected to arm bones, arm bones connected to hand bones, back bones connected to neck bones, neck bones connected to head bones. All the bones were connected. He saw sinews come upon them, and he saw skin cover them. But they were not breathing; they still were not living.

I'm sure Ezekiel must have looked up to God in puzzlement. But God did not keep him puzzled for long. God told Ezekiel to preach to the wind, and he did. Ezekiel told the four winds to breathe upon the bones so that they might live. And as he preached, the breath came into those dry bones that had come together and been covered with sinew, and men stood upon their feet as a great army.

As I read Ezekiel, I began looking at where we live—this community, this country, this nation—and I began to feel as if I were living in a valley of dry bones. I looked around and I saw men and women, boys and girls, deteriorated physically, spiritually, and morally. I saw despair, depression, hunger; I saw the homeless, orphans, and widows by the thousands not being cared for. I saw bloodshed, adultery, extortion, and so much corruption that it caused me to look up to God and wonder, "Can these bones live?" Now I ask this question on three levels: Can your bones live—the individual's? Can our bones live—the community's? Can their bones live—the country's?

I look around at our congregations and some look healthy. And in some the individual members look well, but something seems to be missing. They are just that—individuals, not a congregation, not a church. They have culture but no fire; they have religion but no regeneration. They're dressed fine but they have no life. They know about the sacred things of the church, but they haven't experienced the Holy Spirit. They form new bad habits and leave off old good habits. They make new associations and leave old ones. Their prayer life decreases as their prosperity becomes greater. Their daily communion with God ceases; caring, sharing, and loving dissipate because they just don't have time anymore. I wonder, *Can the individuals' bones live?*

As a community, we lack compassion for one another. Years ago, we as a Black race did not have orphanages, shelter homes, and foster homes filled with our children. We had what are called today "extended families." If a relative died and left children, we took them into our homes and raised them as our own. If there was no family, close friends took them into their homes and raised them. We cared about one another's children. We were interested in their growth. Our parents and grandparents didn't find themselves in nursing homes. We provided for them and cared for them in the warmth of our homes, where they knew that they were being loved and cared for. We didn't leave our responsibilities to the state or the federal government. The church and community took care of their own. I wonder, *Can our community's bones live?*

Our country tries to convince us that we're doing okay. It tells us that the economic depression is over, but we still see that over 50 percent of the unemployment lines are made up of Blacks, because more Black people still have no jobs. Our country tells us we have equal rights. That's what the Constitution says, but we see a difference in how we are treated because of our color or our sex, in some cases because of both. Blacks get arrested and beaten up. Whites get arrested and bailed out. Some Blacks must have a degree to get a decent job, but some Whites don't need a degree; sometimes they don't even need a high school education. Our young men must go into the service because they cannot get jobs. Women are denied opportunities in the secular world and in our churches just because they are women. The 1984 presidential campaign was laden with the fact that Jesse Jackson is Black, not with facts of whether or not he would make a good president. *Can this country's bones live?*

Well, I believe that these bones can live. *My* bones, *your* bones, *our* bones, *the country's* bones can live! They can live if we allow the breath of God to breathe in us. If we who are preachers, teachers, and witnesses of the gospel of Jesus Christ take hold of the vision that was seen by Ezekiel in the valley and are obedient to God and if we preach, pray, and witness with the boldness of Peter, full of the power of God, these bones can live! If we preach and teach and witness about Jesus' hallowed life and the righteousness of his people, these bones can live! If we remind ourselves, our boys and girls, and the country about Martin Luther King, Jr., and his dream of bringing people together—rich, poor, Black, Yellow, and White—these bones can live! If we remember his dream that one day oppression, depression, and degradation will be no more, these bones can live! We will not let his birthday be just another holiday, but Martin Luther King, Jr.'s birthday will symbolize another reason for these bones to live!

If we preach and teach and witness about Jesus and his ascent on high and his triumph over the world and sin, we will know that these bones can live.

Yes, your bones can live if you stop looking at yourself as being the only one that can do a particular job. You know the attitude that some have: "Well, if I don't do it, it won't get done." Another attitude you need to give up is waiting for someone to beg you to use the talents with which God so graciously endowed you. You know what I mean. You have a beautiful voice, but because you can't sing all the lead songs, or because the other choir members are not as spiritual as you are, or because the director doesn't conduct the rehearsal the way you think he or she ought to, you won't sing in the choir. You would make a good Sunday school teacher; you have all the necessary qualifications—willingness to learn the job, willingness to attend the workshops, willingness to share yourself, but because you have to get up early on Sunday morning—the only morning you have to sleep late—you won't teach Sunday school. You're good with figures or you're good with organizing or you are good as a fundraiser, but because you don't want to lend your God-given talent to the church or the community or the nation, you sit back and criticize others who are trying. Some of those who are retired may have the attitude "I've been here all these years, so I should do that" or "I have done my share; let the others do it now." There is no longevity in God's business, and there are no retirements. You may want to change your position and become a consultant or a strong prayer warrior, but you don't stop serving.

Yes, these bones can live. Your bones can live, our bones can live, and the country's bones can live if we put our trust in Jesus and our faith in God.

I'm glad that one day my dry bones had the breath of life breathed into them and became a living soul. I began, then, to understand that if I live for Jesus, everything will be all right. I began to understand what Jesus meant when he said love your neighbor as yourself. I began to understand that I must treat everyone else as I want to be treated, not as they treat me. I learned that to be of service to the Lord, I had to be willing to deny myself, be obedient to God's will, and have God's unconditional love for all people.

Can your bones live? They can if you will follow Jesus. They can if you surrender all to Jesus! They will if you will be like Jesus. Yes, *your bones can live!*

The Survival of the Unfit

Carolyn Ann Knight

While we were still weak, at the right time Christ died for the ungodly. Why, one will hardly die for a righteous man—though perhaps for a good man one will dare even to die. But God shows his love for us in that while we were yet sinners Christ died for us (Romans 5:6-8, RSV).

"To be or not to be, that is the question." What was an existential question for Shakespeare's Hamlet as he stood at the crossroads of his life is, for us today, an ontological question as well. Hamlet's plight of survival is a universal one. In a society that is disgruntled by the contrary winds of desolation and degradation, in a world that is scorched by

Dr. Carolyn Ann Knight is a graduate of Bishop College, Dallas, Texas; of Union Theological Seminary, New York; and of United Theological Seminary of Dayton, Ohio, where she earned the D.Min. She is head of the department of homiletics at the Interdenominational Theological Seminary in Atlanta, Georgia, and in wide demand as a preacher and revivalist across America. She also serves on the advisory board of *The African American Pulpit*, a quarterly journal.

the burning suns of trials and pestilence, in a civilization that is bombarded by the falling rocks of mutilated humanity, we too must grapple with the question "to be or not to be." With each new day that dawns, we stand on the brink of nonexistence.

In America unemployment figures of between eight and eleven million persons are staggering; even more Americans have been forced to stand in cheese and soup lines. More than 32 percent of all Black Americans exist on incomes below the poverty line, and 44 percent of all Black youth live below the poverty line. Modern-day sociologists have painted an even more shocking scenario. They tell us that with the rapid advance of the technological age, it is possible that we are developing a permanent underclass of uneducable, unskilled, and unemployable citizens. Indeed the picture is bleak!

The present administration has budgeted monies in excess of one trillion dollars to increase the nation's military strength. We are told by some military strategists that we are on the threshold of nuclear holocaust, in the event of which all humankind would be erased from the face of the earth. So the question we must answer is even more challenging than the question asked by Hamlet. We must answer not only the question of how we shall survive but also the question of whether we will survive at all.

Natural science raises an interesting issue. Charles Darwin, noted anthropologist and father of the theory of evolution, purported that survival rests in the hands of those who are most capable of surviving—*"the survival of the fittest."* The essence of what he said is this: The strongest man, the richest woman, the smartest young person will make it in life over and against the weak, the poor, and the not so smart. And in this life, that may or may not be the case. One thing we have learned from Reagan's administration and his self-centered brand of economics is that in the 1980s the rich will get richer while the poor get poorer. The haves will have more; the have-nots will have less. We have been continuously frightened by the fierce competition for global superiority between the United States and the Soviet Union—at the expense of innocent men, women and children. Each country pushes and shoves its imperialistic weight around to gain control of the world.

In this materialistic and mundane society in which we live, much value is placed on how strong you are, how rich you are, how smart you are. But I am glad that what Charles Darwin conceived was just theory, for the fact is that it matters not whether you are rich or poor, strong or weak, smart or not smart. These attributes in and of themselves do not qualify you for "fittest" status. They do not guarantee your survival. No, not really. The history pages have reported time and time again the tragic tales of the rich, the strong, and the smart who, confident in these attributes alone, met terrible ends.

The biblical record announces with poignant clarity that it is not always the fittest who will reach the mark and gain the prize. For when we were weak, without strength, when we were in a state of passive helplessness to deliver ourselves from sin, Christ died. At the time in our lives when we were completely disqualified from real existence, Christ died for us. And now, because of Christ, *the unfit survive!* What a paradox! Here is a case in which God almighty favors the underdog. God rises up and fights on the side of the weak, the disadvantaged, and the oppressed. God gives no preferential attention to the high and mighty but has earnest compassion for the meek and lowly.

Who are the unfit? When we really think about it, we find that we are all unfit in many ways. The apostle Paul says, "For all have sinned and come short of the glory of God" (Romans 3:23). There are more unfit than fit, for "there is none righteous, no, not one" (Romans 3:10). God takes all of the unfit and through the tests and trials of life changes that unfitness to mental and spiritual fitness. And we who are the unfit must follow closely the guidelines of divine discipline in order to be best qualified for eternal survival.

There is a word in the fifth chapter of Paul's letter to the church at Rome that speaks of God's miraculous intervention on the part of the unfit. It tells how God pleaded our case—

not when we were at our best, but when humankind was at its very worst: "While we were still weak, at the right time Christ died for the ungodly. Why, one will hardly die for a righteous man—though perhaps for a good man one will dare even to die. But God shows his love for us in that while we were yet sinners Christ died for us" (Romans 5:6-8, RSV).

1. *Survival dictates that we who know ourselves to be unfit be more careful than other people.*

We know without delusion that we have no strength to waste, no ability to squander, no money to throw away. We should be disciplined by our limitations, and therefore, we must move with caution and deliberate intentions. (When we consider the fact that our Social Security resources are about to run dry, we realize that an escalating military budget is even more ridiculous.) We have neither time nor energies to waste on business that is not related to the kingdom of God. The people of God ought to be more prayerful and careful to "work out [their] own salvation with fear and trembling" (Philippians 2:12). We know we are sinners saved by grace. That is why my late and sainted grandmother used to say, "I am sending up my timber every day." She knew that, in order to make it to heaven, she had to be careful of her construction program on earth. That is why every day she would send up *and* out a little faith, hope, and love.

The unfit ought to be more zealous. We know that it takes more effort to survive than not to survive. In order to reach the top, we must climb. The bottom of the ladder of life is cluttered with people who refuse to climb, for climbing requires much effort and preparation. It does not take any effort to reach the bottom, but if we are going to be true Christian citizens, we must climb to the top. Years ago, a noted Bible society was famous for distributing a religious tract that said on the front cover, "What must I do to go to hell?" The answer on the inside was "Nothing!" We do not have to frustrate ourselves, working on all kinds of evil plots and plans to gain admittance to hell; we can just stay as we are and we'll make it! We are already candidates for citizenship in hell. But when Nicodemus asked Jesus a similar question related to the kingdom of God, he received a much different answer. He had asked, "Good Master, what must I do to inherit eternal life?" Jesus told Nicodemus, "You have to do *something* to make it into the kingdom of God. You must have some worthy ambitions and some noble goals. Nicodemus, you must be born again." It requires more to survive than to drift into oblivion.

2. *Survival asserts that endurance is necessary.*

Black people have survived in America, not because they have had the best homes, the best educations, or even the best jobs, but because they have been able to bend with the tests of time rather than break under the strains of life. As a race of people we have survived the snarls of slavery, second-class citizenship, prejudice, and discrimination, not because we had the proper defense, but because on the cotton fields of Georgia, Texas, Mississippi, Alabama, and South Carolina we developed a resilient spirit that was often bent but never broken. If we as a race are to move forward in the cause of humanity, it will not be by our resources alone but by our stamina. We do not have the best of everything now, but God is on our side, and God will see us through. God will open doors, but we must be prepared to enter them. God will give us tasks, and we must be able to get the jobs done.

Accepting insufficiency to the tasks is sacrilegious. Failure to work and to prepare for the work that God has for us is a violation of the gospel prerequisite. God will make a way if the prerequisites have been met. We should rely on God to do the impossible only if we have done what is possible. We should not expect God to give us success if we have not met the requirements for successful living. We should not expect the kingdom of God to come on earth if somewhere during the course of life and living we have not turned our hearts and minds in the kingdom's direction. Giving up and unpreparedness are less than kingdom material.

Here, holding on is the issue. Pressing on is more important than making impressions. Keeping on is more important than keeping up. Our obsession to keep up with individuals, nations, and governments is leading to our rapid destruction.

When we cannot keep up, we can keep on, and God will lift us up. Again, the apostle Paul gives us a guide. In the third chapter of Philippians, Paul says, "Forgetting those things in the past, reaching ahead to new and better things, I press toward the mark for the prize of the high calling of God in Christ Jesus" (vv. 13-14). In writing a letter to his "son" in the ministry, Paul wanted Timothy to know the value of holding on. "Timothy," Paul said, "I have fought the good fight. I did not always win, but I kept on trying. I kept the faith. I finished my course, and now there is laid up for me a crown of life. And not for me only. But for everyone who keeps pressing on" (see 2 Timothy 4:6-8). When you cannot keep up, keep on.

3. *There is eternal survival.*

Though we are unfit for and totally disqualified from God's grace and God's mercy, we are not helpless, and we are not hopeless. When life and living offer us nothing but trouble and despair, God dispatches grace and mercy through clouds of trouble. When storms and convulsive skies are the normal climate of life, God shows his face in the storms of oppression. God rides the waves of the angry sea to save the unfit. God loves us in spite of our incompatibility. Jesus died for us while we were yet unfit. Jesus died in due season, when we could not and would not save ourselves. Christ died for us! When doing good, living right, and following the law offered no hope for atonement or salvation, Jesus died for us. But make no mistake about it—his death was not without purpose: "For God so loved the world that he gave his only Son, that whoever believes in him should not perish but have eternal life." Jesus did not die that we might remain unfit. He died that we might be made fit, that we might achieve, that we might gain strength to become peacemakers, that we might be called the sons and the daughters of God. Jesus died that we might reap in due season. When the harvest is ripe, we shall come rejoicing, bringing our restored lives with us.

John the Revelator saw two crowds entering into the kingdom of God. The first crowd was the 144,000—the chosen nation, the expected, advantaged crowd. The first crowd was recognized and named: Benjamin, Reuben, Judah, Asher, Naphtali, and so on. But they were not all who would inherit eternity. Right behind that crowd, John saw also a nameless host of unfit people coming along—some crippled, some crawling, some bleeding—broken, scarred, and wounded. Who are these? They are not the "fittest." These are not members of the Twelve Tribes of Israel. These are they that have come up out of great tribulation. These are they "who fought to win the prize and sailed through bloody seas." These are they who suffered but now reign. They were dead, but now they live. They were crippled, but now they are whole. They were wounded, but now they are healed. They were oppressed and downcast, but now they are free. Yes! These are they who have washed their robes in the blood of the precious Lamb! Yes! I want to be in that crowd. God will be our God, and we shall be his people—and God shall wipe away all tears from our eyes. I want to be in that number when the saints go marching in.

> When the saints go marching in,
>   Oh, when the saints go marching in;
> Lord, I want to be in that number,
>   when the saints go marching in.
>
> When they march around God's throne,
>   Oh, when they march around God's throne;
> Lord, I want to be in that number,
>   when they march around God's throne.
>
> When they crown Him Lord of Lords,
>   Oh, when they crown Him Lord of Lords;
> Lord, I want to be in that number,
>   when they crown Him Lord of Lords.

To Set at Liberty

Deborah McGill-Jackson

And he came to Nazareth, where he had been brought up;
and he went to the synagogue, as his custom was, on the
sabbath day. And he stood up to read; and there was given
to him the book of the prophet Isaiah. He opened the book
and found the place where it was written,
"The Spirit of the Lord is upon me,
because he has anointed me to preach good news to the poor.
He has sent me to proclaim release to the captives
and recovering of sight to the blind,
to set at liberty those who are oppressed,
to proclaim the acceptable year of the Lord."

Dr. Deborah McGill-Jackson, an ordained American Baptist minister, is a graduate of Brown University, Providence, and holds masters degrees from the Samuel Proctor School of Theology, Virginia Union University, and the Presbyterian School of Christian Education, both in Richmond, Virginia. Previously a professor at Norfolk State University and on the staff of the First Baptist Church of Norfolk, Virginia, she is now relocated to Detroit, Michigan.

And he closed the book, and gave it back to the attendant, and sat down; and the eyes of all in the synagogue were fixed on him (Luke 4:16-20, RSV).

The conviction of the Lukan passage has both a universal and a particular focus for those of us that would study the word of God and attempt to live by it. The context in which the subject "to set at liberty" is placed delineates both our quest as individuals called into relationship with Jesus Christ and our task as servants of that same Christ and his people whose corporate witness makes evident the liberation of social structures and institutions. How awesome the work; how frail and feeble the workers! Still, the spirit of the declaration and its impact upon those in whose company these words were uttered call us to self-examination as well as to a closer examination of the text. We are convicted as we realize the limited expression of what we are and what we have done in light of all that God has blessed us with and calls us to do.

"And he came to Nazareth, where he had been brought up, and he went to the synagogue, as his custom was, on the sabbath day. And he stood up to read; and there was given to him the book of the prophet Isaiah. He opened the book and found the place where it was written. . . ." Is there significance in the fact that this Jesus of Nazareth was at home, in his home church (as it were), following the custom of his day—when these poignant words were read anew by one who later declared their fulfillment resided within Jesus? Some might suggest that Jesus' presence here signified the importance of the need of self-affirmation, which we must all meet before beginning our life's quest. By first recognizing from whence we've come, we can then proceed on the journey towards transformation. Surely, we are told in Luke 4 that Jesus—having been baptized by the Holy Spirit and led by the Spirit into the wilderness, and having then returned—proceeded to teach in the synagogues throughout the surrounding country. But it was upon his return home that he made a pronouncement of his calling. He identified himself as being in relationship to the Eternal and called into relationship with the poor, the captive, the blind, and the oppressed. Can we not agree that Jesus' coming to Nazareth was similar to his coming into our lives as the Christ? Perhaps Jesus was aware of the need of the people in this village to know of him both as he was and as he was becoming—completely transformed by the Spirit within him. Perhaps the Nazarenes, having known him as he grew up, now needed to hear this man, this "son" of Joseph and Mary, declare the true understanding of his being.

Likewise, we stand in need of a transformed perspective of who the Christ is and what the presence of the Christ in our lives can mean. How difficult it is to accept the truth when we are confronted by the Christ! Quite often we have labored long—under the false pretense that we know who we are and that the world offers us freedom—only to discover the limitedness of our understanding. We are held captive by the whims and fancies of this world and our self-centered existence. Jesus went to Nazareth as the Liberator par excellence, revealing the truth and promising liberation. Jesus came declaring a program for liberation as the content of his ministry in, to, and with the world. Christians are called to participate in the liberation of others, for we have become heirs of the message of freedom and inheritors of the liberation agenda.

The world is still in need of hearing and living out the word of freedom. The world is in need of liberation, for there are among us those poor in spirit and in material substance. Are not men and women held captive by their past? Are they not ashamed and guilt ridden? Is not the society caught in its own web of greed and abuse? Are there not among us those blind to the truth declared in love and overshadowed by ignorance of spirit? Are there not among us those who would oppress? Are we not frequently participants in the oppression of others on the basis of religion, race, wealth, sex, and nationality?

Is not the cry for liberation also felt in our bosoms, and is this not the goal of our journey in Christ? The Scriptures tell us, "And they handed to him the book, and he read: 'The Spirit of the Lord is upon me, because he has anointed me to preach good news to the poor. He has sent me to proclaim release to the captives and recovering of sight to the blind.'" The word heard that day highlighted the urgency of the task of the proclamation of giving life to the word preached and found in the task "to set at liberty those who are oppressed." For Christians this summarizes the whole agenda for liberation.

The significance of this call to ministry, this challenge for ministry, would be overwhelming for us today if it were not for the One who went before. Jesus Christ as the forerunner of our labors and our struggles is the one who shows us the way and is, in fact, the way to all truth. He demonstrated the power and authority of the most high God as he went forth into the highways and byways to heal the sick, to comfort the brokenhearted, to preach the Good News to the poor, and to set at liberty all who were captive. We must do likewise, individually and collectively, as we acknowledge the Spirit within us and upon us. We have been anointed for a purpose and made ready to share in the liberation of the people of God as followers of Christ.

What, then, is the nature of this challenge for ministry to set at liberty? How are we to participate in the consummation of all human hope, to experience transformation, while proclaiming the past and sharing in the future? How are we somehow to use the symbols of the tradition for the liberation of a people over whom the tradition has often been used as an instrument of oppression? How are we—the feeble, the frail, the ignorant, the proud, the sinful, the outcast, and the leftover—to transcend what was and what is, in order to be transformed by what can be? Unless we identify who we are in light of *whose* we are and submit to the Spirit's power to mold, melt, and make us; unless we stand in the churches of our day, as did Jesus, acknowledging the Spirit and not our possessions; unless the presence of God is made evident in our sermons, our prayers, and our lives; then liberation cannot take place through us. Rather, it will be hindered by us, and a "ministry" of oppression, prejudice, and self-righteousness will tell our story and debase the gospel for which Jesus lived and died.

But let us be assured that when we give ourselves to the power and work of the Spirit, a new identity will be given us—not "Saul" but "Paul"—because God has called us to a holy work and set us aside to be a people prepared to minister to those in need of liberation. The time is too short and the suffering too great for us to spend all our time discussing the appropriateness of liberation and refusing to take the risks of involving and engaging the oppressive institutions, people, and ideologies. The time is at hand for the saved, the "being saved," and the "shall be saved" to lift high the banner of salvation, to carry it into the trenches of human sin, despair, and hopelessness, and to reclaim the offspring of the Creator in the name of Christ. We dare not put on blinders to avoid viewing the realities of the masses. We in the church cannot afford to reject the gospel that convicts us in our comfort. The church must loosen the shackles by which it is bound—the shackles of tradition, the irons of prejudice, the bars of isolation and suburban escapism—lest church people and their ecclesiastical palaces deteriorate in their own captivity, which is due to the sin of alienation.

The day of release must not be far off. The spiritually and physically blind wait, frightened by terrors unseen; the blinded soul and blinded eye are entombed in hopelessness and faithlessness. Soon we will become sinfully content in our forms of blind piety, and we will not permit the true light of Christ to pierce our darkness. Comfort and contentment will cause us to atrophy spiritually. Our faith and works will amount to nothing before God. A nation blind to the hungry, the poor, and the aged will make security its object of faith and the mounting of destructive instruments its "works." A people blind to their own beauty will feed upon their own members, never confronting the institutions, persons, and philosophies that hold them, as a people, captive. A church blind to its true mission will cultivate division within its walls, rather than ministry to and with its naked, imprisoned, and oppressed neighbors. Individuals blind to the truth about themselves will be unable to face the potential that transcends their previous failures and faults. Unless someone proclaims the truth that can pierce the darkness, the sightless will remain captive. Unless someone delivers the empowered radiance of righteousness that can overcome the corrosive and destructive forces of unrighteousness, the creation will remain captive. Many will choose to remain in bondage to the fallacy of human security and self-gratification at the expense of others. These people will willingly oppress others and delay the coming kingdom of God, the kingdom realized in all its glory.

But it will not always be like this. The powers opposed to the will of God will not prevail, for it has been ordained that a remnant shall exist. This remnant, faithfully striving through briny tears and with calloused limbs—though they know weeping in the midnight hour—will know joy in the morning. People of this remnant will seek liberation wherever oppression is found. They will not be turned back or persuaded to do less. They will gladly accept the risks for the sake of freedom rather than be comfortable in the security of the world, for in their hearts they know only one place where peace and rest may be found—in the bosom of God. The people of the remnant know their destiny and the way by which that destiny shall be reached, for Jesus Christ is the way, the truth, and the life. The Spirit anointed him to preach the Good News, to proclaim release to the captive, and to give sight to the blind, in other words, to set at liberty. Jesus Christ is the Liberator, for he brought the Good News of redemption, salvation, and liberation. He brought both a word to transcend and a will to transform the afflicted and the afflictions of poverty of spirit and of body. This same Jesus has placed in the hands of the remnant people the keys of release, the balm for healing, the word that liberates. In the footprints of Jesus, the supreme Liberator, they are called to walk, and the way they are to walk. We are "they," the people of the remnant church, called to set at liberty the poor and the rich, the oppressed and the oppressor, the mind and the body. We are called to set at liberty the bigot and the chauvinist, whose self-understanding must be engaged by the transforming power of the Holy Spirit through our witness, whereby they may know freedom apart from the enslavement of another. We are called to set at liberty a nation—under God, indivisible, where justice and freedom belong to all God's children—so that justice may roll down like waters and righteousness like an everflowing stream. We are called to set at liberty a world bent on self-destruction rather than the construction of peace. Such power to bring liberation—to set at liberty the blind, the poor, the captive, and the oppressed—is ours by appropriating the mind-set to receive it and the lifestyle to use it, not for the praise of men and women, but for the glory of God.

The acceptable year of the Lord is now. It was actualized when people heard the Good News, and, as Isaiah envisioned (in chapter 61), it brought comfort to all who mourned; it gave a garland instead of ashes, the oil of gladness instead of mourning, the mantle of praise instead of a faint spirit. Those once captive were called oaks of righteousness; those that were poor obtained the keys to the kingdom, the blind beheld a new understanding. Where sin had bestowed shame, a double portion of forgiveness became a reason to rejoice; where robbery and wrong had ruled, love and justice conquered. Not just in hearing, but in doing was liberation realized. Thus our task, our purpose, our ministry is to keep the living Word ever before the people. We know for ourselves that once we were in shackles and then we heard the Word. We were moved and convicted by the Word. Our lives were acted upon by the Word. Now we have a witness that once we were bowed down, brow furled, heart heavy from sin, sorrow, and oppression—and we were met by the Christ and invited to know what joy was all about, a joy the world cannot give and cannot take away. I'm glad I know the Christ for myself and have experienced the liberating power of Jesus in my life. There are still times when I am among the poor in spirit, when I am held captive by my past. Even though the road has been rugged and the way gets weary, I hear the

Word promise freedom in the midst of struggle. And I'm glad that as I strive to follow Christ, empowered by the Holy Spirit and surrounded with the precious love of God, I can respond to an agenda for liberation, peace, and love. I can be certain because something inside is giving me the assurance that these days are not in vain and that we will know liberation. We will be set at liberty—set free from the tears, set free from the trials, set free from the tribulations and the storms.

We will be set at liberty from the prejudices, sins, and struggles of this old world, and we will behold a new heaven and a new earth. Someday we'll *know* what we've only glimpsed—full freedom in God, whose glory will be manifested all around. On that great consummation day all will gather, lifting their voices; earth and heaven will ring true with the harmonies of liberty.

But until that day arrives, we're called, not only to preach the Good News in season and out of season, but also to set at liberty the poor, the captive, the blind, and the oppressed. Until that day we must proclaim the Good News in word and deed.

On Remembering Who We Are

Katie G. Cannon

Genesis 21:1-21, the culmination of a story about a struggle between two women—Sarah and Hagar—is the basis of my message. Let me provide some background for the struggle. Sarah and Hagar had many differences stemming from the fact that one was free and the other enslaved. At the beginning of the story in Genesis 16:1, we learn that Sister Hagar had been uprooted from her homeland in Egypt. She was snatched from her African heritage. Abraham paid money and brought Hagar into his household as a slave.

Because she was a slave, Hagar was denied the God-given

Dr. Katie G. Cannon is the Annie Scales Rogers Chair in Social Ethics at Union Theological Seminary, Richmond, Virginia. A graduate of Barber Scotia College, Concord, North Carolina, and of Johnson C. Smith Theological Seminary at the Interdenominational Theological Center in Atlanta, Georgia, she earned her Ph.D. at Union Theological Seminary, New York City. A member of *The African American Pulpit* advisory board, she is a frequent author and widely heard lecturer and preacher.

rights of her humanity. Hagar was given burdensome tasks, lowly and menial jobs, and the most difficult work to do. In addition, she was forced to work under the strict supervision of Sarah, who was the legal wife of Abraham and, therefore, the madam of the household.

In spite of the differences between Hagar and Sarah, one of the important things that these two women had in common was the fact that they each had given birth to a child of the same man, which I am sure added to the intense conflict between them.

Sarah had waited a long, long time in order to be God's instrument in carrying out God's promise to Abraham. God had promised Abraham that if he would go from his country, if he would leave his kinfolk, if he would leave all that was familiar to him and go to an unknown land where God would direct him, then Abraham would become a great nation, through which all the families of the earth would be blessed. But even though God had made this promise, Sarah was barren.

Now Sarah interpreted her barrenness as a stumbling block to God. God had said that Abraham's descendents would outnumber the stars in the heavens. Abraham's descendents would match in number the grains of sand on the seashore. And yet, Sarah and Abraham still were not parents.

So, the Bible says, Sarah decided that she would take matters into her own hands and help God keep God's own promise. Like Sarah, when we think that God is moving too slow on what we want in our lives, we try to take charge of the situation. We not only try to dictate our lives but we also attempt to serve as dictators in the lives of those around us. This is exactly what Sarah did.

Following the customs and traditions of her day, Sarah tried to assist God out of what she saw to be God's dilemma by offering the slave woman Hagar to her husband, Abraham, so that he might be the father of at least one child before he died. Being a slave, Hagar had no say in this matter. Abraham was eighty-six years old when Hagar served as his surrogate wife. She conceived and gave birth to Abraham's first child, a son called Ishmael, whose name means "God hears."

As our background concludes, Sarah had become extremely jealous of Hagar and her baby. Sarah could not deal with
the fact that the slavewoman had played a greater role than
she had in realizing God's promise.

In Genesis 21, our text, we see that eventually, when Abraham was about one hundred years old, Sarah, too, bore a
child, a son who was named Isaac, meaning, "May God
laugh—may God look benevolently upon you."

Even though Sarah had her own child, she remained insanely jealous of Hagar, treating her harshly. So Sarah nagged
Abraham. She fussed and pouted. Sarah pitched all kinds of
temper tantrums, insisting that Hagar and Ishmael be cast
into the wilderness. And that is exactly what Abraham did;
he gave in to Sarah's wishes and sent Hagar and Ishmael
away from his household with only meager rations on which
to survive.

The last verses of our text say that while Hagar was crying
and praying and praying and crying, God heard her and the
cries of her child, Ishmael: "And the angel of God called to
Hagar from heaven, and said to her, 'What troubles you,
Hagar? Fear not, for God has heard. . . .'" (Genesis 21:17,
RSV). Yes, God took full responsibility to fill their every need.

We now come to our subject—"On Remembering Who We
Are." Sisters and brothers, I ask you, how are we just like
Abraham? Where in our lives can we identify with the character of Sarah? What can we learn from Hagar so that our
own living will not be in vain?

Our concern is the tendency that many of us have to overstep
our boundaries as human beings; we try to take the serious
matters of life into our own hands because we forget our
identity as finite beings. By this I mean that as Christians we
often suffer from a spiritual identity crisis; that is, we are self-
righteous, egotistical, judgmental or extremely perfectionistic
with ourselves and our loved ones because we lose touch
with who is really the true and living God in our lives. What
I am saying is that as long as we continue spinning our
wheels, trying to change people, trying to change places,

trying to change things we can*not* change, and as long as we sit idly by in self-pity and apathy because we lack courage to change the things we *can*, then we will continue to lack the wisdom, which comes from God, that helps us to know the difference.

For instance, as Black women (and as Black men) some of us get caught up in the Abraham syndrome of becoming great people pleasers. We avoid conflict at all costs. For example, Abraham knew better than to usurp God's promise and have a child by Hagar, and yet he acquiesced to the pressures of Sarah and did wrong. We, too, as grandmothers and mothers, as sisters and daughters, as aunts and nieces, receive as part of our socialization as Black females growing up in a racist White society the notion that we are supposed to take care of everybody except ourselves. As with Abraham, God has a special job for each of us to do. And yet, many of us mess ourselves up over and over again by giving in to the pressures around us to do what we know in our heart of hearts to be wrong; and this happens because we get caught up into the Abraham syndrome of people pleasing. We forget who we are.

Again, others of us, as Black women and Black men in the church, suffer from the Sarah syndrome and try to be little false gods to those around us. Far too many Black women spend their whole lives in the church and never get religion, never experience an active faith or a loving God because they are so busy controlling the Spirit of God that moves within, the Spirit that gives them meaning. Some of us in marriages, relationships, families, and friendships have not yet learned that we have no power to change and to make over grown folks. But whenever we get caught in the Sarah syndrome, we snatch back our lives and our wills from God and we try by hook or by crook to make people do what we want them to do. When we are suffering from this syndrome, we pray that our will be done instead of humbly surrendering ourselves before God and asking that God's will be done in our own lives and also in the lives of those we love and care about.

And the serious danger with living out our days in either the Abraham syndrome of people pleasing or in the Sarah syndrome of trespassing on God's territory is that we forget that we are sisters of Hagar and that God hears our prayers. The social and medical statistics bear out the evidence that Black women are rushing to premature graves in larger numbers than ever before as a result of this spiritual bankruptcy. More Black women than ever are dying from strokes, high-blood-pressure diseases, and heart attacks. More than ever we are victims of chronic depression, nervous breakdowns, and schizophrenic behavior. The number of Black women suffering from alcoholism, drug abuse, and compulsive substance consumption has reached an all-time high. Too many sisters are dying with broken hearts, broken minds, and broken spirits, not knowing who they truly are.

Therefore, since we see how these Abraham and Sarah syndromes will cause spiritual bankruptcy and since we see how they will rush us to a premature grave, let us embrace three elements related to remembering who we are in order that we may grow to be the full persons that God has created each of us to be.

The first element we need to embrace related to remembering who we are is the element of *willingness*. We must be willing to find our oneness with God in order to know our true identity. To say that our identity is in a God who gives us free will is to say that God knows our thoughts, that God knows all our "goings out" and our "comings in" and yet God gives us the freedom to choose what we want. Each and every day that we live, we are free to choose right or to choose wrong. God gives us the freedom to choose good or to choose evil. But the gift we must not forget is the gift of choice.

Sister Hagar, when cast into the wilderness with her child, Ishmael, chose to cry out a prayer in the name of the living God. When we are hurting and in trouble or when we feel downtrodden and abused, we too need to remember that we can turn our lives and wills over to the care of God and have the faith to believe that God will hear our prayers.

Willingness requires that we let go of our self-imposed imprisonments. Revelation 3:20 tells us that, behold, the Lord stands at the door of our hearts knocking, and if any one hears and opens the door, the Lord will come in to that person and be with him or her. This is what the first element is all about. In remembering who we are, we must recall that unless we are willing to open up the door of our hearts, God cannot come in. In order for us to be free of the Abraham syndrome and the Sarah syndrome, we must be willing to let God into our lives. As the familiar saying goes, we must be able to "let go and let God" be the master of our fate and the captain of our souls. For when we allow our wills to conform to God's will, then and only then do we begin to know who we truly are.

Now, the second element we need to embrace related to remembering who we are is the element of *humility*. As Christians, in order for us to receive God's blessings, we must humble ourselves before almighty God, morning by morning and day by day. We need to realize that the kind of humility that strengthens us for the struggles before us is not abject subservience. Nor is it awe at the greatness of others. The kind of humility that I am talking about is not the dramatic put-down of ourselves wherein we exaggerate all the mistakes and sins of our past. Christian humility does not mean being completely submissive, wallowing and shuffling, putting everyone else on a pedestal, and accepting everything that comes our way.

Instead, the kind of humility that refreshes our souls so that we can run on and see what the end is going to be is the humility that lets us accept with clarity *what* we are and *who* we are, followed by a sincere attempt to become who God has created us to be.

What I am saying here is this: as clergy and laity, as church officers and choir members, as young and old worshipers—all of us who are baptized Christians—when we embrace humility, we take the risk to have a level look at our real selves as to where we stand in relation to God and in relation to others. Humility forces us to let go of the raw hurts and the ragged delusions. Humility encourages us to reach out to the Power outside our limited, finite selves.

According to our text, this is the kind of humility that Hagar had. Even though she was a slavewoman, according to the Hebrew codes, Hagar had certain rights of protection as the mother of Abraham's son. She chose not to lean on the law; she chose neither to retaliate nor to seek revenge.

The same lesson is true for us today. If we are serious about living faithful lives as Christians, then we need to make the practice of humility a part of our daily living. There will be times when we, too, will have the opportunity to get revenge against those who oppose us, those who oppress us, those who inflict all manner of evil against us; and it is during these times that we need to cry out with humility like Sister Hagar and find out what specific action God is revealing to us each day.

I believe that this second element, humility, allows God to work through us with good words. Humility allows God to work through us with good thoughts. Humility allows God to work through us with good deeds so that we can know who we truly are.

Now, the third and final element we need to embrace related to remembering who we are is the element of *openmindedness*. Openmindedness requires us to seek to understand others rather than always trying to be understood. After we have surrendered our will to the care of God, and embraced a new quality of humility, then the last step calls for us to respect the different ways in which we all walk, talk, and have our being. Dearly beloved, let us never be so rigid as to discount another's lifestyle in ministry of the church. There are no hard-and-fast, one-hundred-percent-foolproof ways to do the work of the Lord. We must use what's best for us at a particular time, keeping our minds open regarding the kinds of help we may find valuable at another time. Each of us needs to develop a receptive attitude that allows us to listen, to learn, and to love. Openmindedness makes us less hasty in drawing judgmental conclusions about our sisters and our brothers. With open minds we not only grow but we also grow up, maturing in our faith as God-fearing people.

The Scriptures tell us that Hagar's faith produced in her an open mind. After all the water Abraham had given her was gone, Hagar put the child under a bush and went off about the distance of a bow-shot and fell down and prayed, opening her soul to God. In Hagar's prayer it is clear that she sought to understand rather than to be understood. Because Hagar was open to the provisions from God, God caused a spring of fresh water to appear in the desert for Hagar and her child.

When we have open minds, we are aware of the springs of fresh and living water in the desert places in our lives. In remembering who we are, we must recall that we belong to a living God who seeks to save, to reconcile, and to claim us as God's own.

There used to be a poster at Union Seminary in New York City that read, "If you had five minutes to live, who would you call and tell them you love them? Why wait until the last five minutes of your life?" I ask this now. Why wait until the last five minutes of our lives to express openly to people how much we love them? If we know of a sister or a brother— wandering around lost unto herself or himself—who doesn't know which way to turn or where to go, who is bent on self-destruction and cut off from the joy of living because she or he has been cast out into the wilderness of life, then let us open ourselves to the Spirit of God so that we can help provide the spiritual water that that sister or brother needs to come back home. Let us open ourselves to the grace of God and share the many blessings that God has bestowed upon us. This third element, openmindedness, lends itself to openheartedness so that we can know who we truly are.

In closing I challenge you to go forth remembering who you are. You are persons created in God's own image. You are sisters of Hagar. And, when in doubt, simply recall the word *WHO—W* for willingness, *H* for humility and *O* for openmindedness—and the God that we serve, the true and living God, has promised to hear your prayers. Amen.

Singing the Lord's Song

Yvonne V. Delk

In Psalm 137 these words are recorded:

> By the waters of Babylon,
> there we sat down and wept,
>   when we remembered Zion.
> On the willows there
>   we hung up our lyres.
> For there our captors
>   required of us songs,
> and our tormentors, mirth, saying,
>   "Sing us one of the songs of Zion!"
> *How shall we sing the LORD's song in a foreign land?*
>   —vv.1-4 (RSV, emphasis added)

The Israelites had been removed by force from their home-

Dr. Yvonne V. Delk recently retired as area executive for the United Church of Christ in Chicago. Prior to that she was the denomination's national executive director of the Office for Church in Society, with offices in New York City. She received degrees from Norfolk State University, Virginia; Andover Newton Theological School, Massachusetts; and New York Theological Seminary, New York City. She is nationally known for her work in affirmative action and as an education specialist to black and urban churches. She travels extensively as lecturer and preacher.

land, Zion. They were broken, out of touch with their roots, their identity, and their God. They were in a strange land. The psalmist pictured them sitting by the waters of Babylon. While Zion was the city of salvation, Babylon was the city of death. In Zion there were community, reconciliation, freedom, and peace, but in Babylon there were alienation and hardness of heart. Babylon's god was power, greed, materialism, selling, and buying; religion was instituted to justify and camouflage Babylon's motives. But the people of Zion were not deceived, for when they remembered Zion—their true ground, the source of their being, the place of their wholeness and renewal—they sat down as mourners. They had no heart for music or song.

The cause of this sad scene as the psalmist described it, was the heartless request of the Israelites' captors—those who had enslaved them—to sing for them one of the songs of Zion. Perhaps their masters had heard reports of the temple music of Zion, or perhaps they wished, like other conquerors in history, to extract some amusement from the native songs of the captives.

But for the exiles there were no songs of Zion but the Lord's songs. The songs of Zion were not the songs of patriotism or nationalism. They were the songs of the Creator, who alone calls worlds into being and sets before us the ways of life and death. It was this recognition that forced the exiles to cry out, "How shall we sing the LORD's song in a foreign land?"

Over two thousand years have passed since the psalmist gave expression to that question. And yet people of faith still wrestle with the question as they attempt to be faithful witnesses in the midst of the issues of our day. The seventies and the eighties have been times of despair for men, women, youth, and children. The experiences of many in our nation can be compared to the Babylonian experience described in Psalm 137. Many people are existing in what can be called a time of "Code Blue." "Code Blue" is a hospital term used to place all hospital personnel on alert. It is a signal of an emergency or a danger of cosmic proportions. It is a signal that alerts staff to the fact that large numbers of persons have been injured and are in life-threatening situations.

We are living in a time of extreme danger and emergency. It is a time when the survival of people is at stake, when millions of people are out of work, and when many members of our community—the poor—are being denied the right to eat. It is a time of "Code Blue" when one million people have been made ineligible for food stamps and the system denies children access to health care and food for their bodies. For instance, tens of thousands of children have lost Medicaid coverage, and hundreds of thousands of poor youngsters no longer receive free or reduced-price lunches. It is a time of "Code Blue" when we deny nutritional and health support systems to women, infants, and children at a time when Black infants are twice as likely as White infants to die within the first year of life. It is a time of "Code Blue" when men, women, and children are sacrificed on the altar of a military god—by those who believe that national security, respect, and pride can be built by creating more and more armaments. It is a time of "Code Blue" when we face the reality of a nuclear war.

People are frightened about the consequences of a nuclear war because they know there would be no winners. Few people would survive. People are marching to protest nuclear arms. People are marching to affirm the right to life for themselves and their children. It is a time of "Code Blue" when the Klan still marches boldly in our midst. It is a time of "Code Blue" when violence and injustice become accepted as a part of the daily fabric of life. In this Babylonian-like time of "Code Blue," *how do we sing the Lord's song?* Will the times in which we live wear us down?

I am afraid that we will fall prey to one of four basic evils as anxiety, confusion, and complexity settle in among us.

There is the danger of becoming a private and narcissistic person. That is, we become "I" persons who turn inward, losing a grounding in community, losing the sense of collective responsibility for being good neighbors. What takes the place of this awareness is a moral vacuum; others are forever trapped in private destinies, doomed to whatever befalls them. In that void the traditional measure of justice or good vanishes completely; the self replaces community, relationships, neighbors, or God.

There is the danger of becoming cynical and disillusioned and settling for the status quo. We give up. We are trapped into believing that it doesn't matter what we do, that things will never change. We merely survive; we simply get by with a minimum of effort.

There is a danger of becoming a ritualistic dancer. That is, we become blind to the conditions around us and keep on with our daily petty routines as if nothing matters. We block out the reality of the world with rituals that consume our time and our energy. We join social clubs to escape; we watch television to escape; we become joggers and runners to escape; we become obsessed with "things" as a way to escape. Our dancing, however, only creates false illusions, meaningless activity, and empty images as we hide behind masks.

There is the danger that we will retreat to simple places and easy answers. "Simple places" means to go back to the "good old days." Gladys Knight reminds us that time has a way of changing things. We glorify the past as a means of escaping from the present. The other retreat is into easy answers. Yet the journey of faith sometimes leads us to the unknown; it leads us away from the simplicity of easy answers, visible enemies, and the assurances that we are right to the complexity of a world where our faith becomes a verb and not simply a noun.

The question we face as Christians is "How do we sing the Lord's song in the midst of the world's evils?" By becoming closed and private? By becoming disillusioned and cynical? By engaging in ritualistic dances? By escaping into a simple place and time? By seeking easy answers? What is it that keeps us anchored and focused in the midst of the "Code Blues" so that we can sing the Lord's song? Permit me to answer with a parable and three affirmations.

During a performance in observance of the birthday of Martin L. King, Jr., I witnessed a ballet performed by children. The ballet was interpreted by a group of choral readers who were reciting a poem by Owen Dodson. In the ballet the children danced out the journey of struggle, survival, despair, and hope as they moved toward the land of the great mountains, a fertile land which held promise and opportunity for all. They moved in their journey through periods of doubt and disbelief. At times they seemed to be lost; they were on unfamiliar ground and the road seemed unchartered. They told stories while on the journey. The stories reminded them of who they were, of the power that surrounded them and the reason they were traveling. After what appeared to be a long and tiresome journey, they finally caught a glimpse of the "promised land"—the land of the great mountains. However, as they came closer to the land of their dreams, they realized that a chasm separated them from the promise. It was clear that if they were to reach the land of the great mountains, they had to cross the chasm.

The more they looked at the chasm, the more anxious and fearful they became. They knew the danger. They needed a word of hope. And so they regrouped. They retold the story, and the story gave them identity, purpose, and power. Suddenly, in an act of faith, one of them positioned herself, took the risk, and leaped into the air. As the child leaped, she reached forward toward the land of the great mountains and she reached back in an act of solidarity and empowerment to grasp the hand of a brother to take with her. He followed her example while holding onto her hand. He reached back and clasped the hand of a sister to take with him, and suddenly, the stage exploded with a human chain leaping over the chasm to the land of the great mountains. It was a triumphant moment.

However, the joy of the moment was interrupted. A crisis occurred. As the last person prepared for the leap, she put down her baby in order to get a firmer grip on her before they moved across the chasm. However, the momentum of the human chain reached her before she was ready. Her hand was grasped, and before she could grasp her child, she was taken over the chasm. Her child was left—alone—on the other side. The child became fearful and anxious. A chasm separated her from her mother, her people, her hope, her future. She wandered in her anxiety toward the edge of the chasm. However, the community called to her. They called her by name. They told her the story. They encouraged her to leap. I watched with a joy I could hardly contain as the child gathered courage and confidence and was empowered by the community. Keeping her eyes on the great mountains, she leaped into the air over the chasm and into the arms of the waiting community.

There was an old man sitting in the audience. Suddenly, it was no longer a play for him. It was real. He rushed to the stage, picked up the child, held her high in the air, and proclaimed with the voice of wisdom and vision, "Thank God almighty! Even our children know how to fly!" We *can* sing the Lord's song if we remember who we are, if we know what we stand for, and if we realize that God's people, God's songs, and God's word are for Babylon as well as for Zion.

We can sing God's song if we remember who we are. Our task as Christians is to keep clearly before all persons who they are and under whose banner they are marching. *We are God's people.* We are authorized, anointed, or given our authority, not by Reagan, Reagonomics, budgets, or events, but by God. Our spirituality is rooted in God. We can sing God's song because we know we are rooted in God. We can sing God's song because we know that Someone who doesn't use star charts, horoscopes, or stock market predictions has a vision in determining who we are and who we shall be.

This blessed assurance keeps us from the danger of hopelessness. It liberates us from the Babylonian experience of racism, sexism, classism, or militarism. In order to sing God's song, we begin by confessing God as our ground, first, foremost, and always. God becomes to us not simply a psychological feeling but the one who authored us, who breathed into us the breath of life, and who calls us daily into community with the Creator and with our sisters and brothers. It is God, not events, who gives us the song that we can sing.

We are a people with a story and with a history of experiences; we must keep our story before us as a way of grounding and rooting ourselves. We must keep telling the stories that remind us of who we are. Storytelling is a way of inviting persons to share in a covenanting mission consciousness. The children in the ballet made it over the chasm because they told stories that reminded them of who they were. My family and I made it through the roughest part of our existence because we had support, the nurturing love of a faith community who reminded us every Sunday morning of our identity: "You are children of God." Whenever two or three of us gather together in the name of Jesus Christ, it ought to be the occasion for telling the story of who we are as God's people.

We can sing God's song if we know what we stand for. Telling our story provides us with a standing ground, a mission, and a practical agenda for our lives that we are not free to walk away from. We can sing God's song if we understand that the demand of the gospel is that we struggle with and on behalf of those who are poor and dispossessed.

Jesus' head and heart were finely tuned to those in need. He healed on the sabbath. Because there was a need, he touched people who had leprosy and a woman who had an issue of blood. Rules, rituals, customs, and even the priests of the temple did not prevent him from being God's new Word in an old world that was still held in captivity and bondage by the powers and principalities of rulers and managers.

The radical demand of the gospel is that we take up the cross and follow Christ. The cross always precedes the crown. There is no victory without struggle. We are therefore called to risk our names, our titles, our degrees, our positions, our statuses, and yes, even our faith for the vision of a world where justice, liberty, and wholeness prevail. When we risk in the name of justice, we sing God's song. When we risk in the name of healing for the broken, we sing God's song. To sing God's song in this decade can require no less than a strong commitment against racism, sexism, and classism, shown by our words and actions. We must be cautious about treating any institution as final, defining any idea as infallible, or accepting any system as closed.

We can sing the Lord's song if we understand a simple but very basic truth: The Lord's song was created not only for Zion but for Babylon as well. We are called to sing God's song wherever people feel trapped, wherever they are hurting, oppressed, or struggling under overwhelming life-denying circumstances. The most powerful song that was ever sung was heard from a cross. However, that cross produced a crown and a symbol for life over death. Persons who have struggled and who know something about pain and how to overcome it can sing God's songs. Those who have been in the valley of the shadow of death can sing the songs of Zion with power and meaning.

Black people know about singing God's song in a strange and foreign land because Black Americans' spirituality was born in the context of the struggle for justice. We sang our songs on boats called *Jesus* that brought us to America. We sang our songs on auction blocks—"Over my head I hear music in the air; there must be a God somewhere." We sang our songs on plantations—"Walk together children, don't you get weary; there is a camp meeting in the promised land." We sang our songs on picket lines—"Ain't gonna let nobody turn me around, I'm gonna keep on marching, keep on praying, keep on singing, moving to the freedom land." We have sung our songs as we moved through the past 367 years. At times the journey was like a sojourn in Babylon; however, we kept on moving from the wilderness of our past and present to the promise and hope of our future.

How can you sing God's song in the midst of the "Code Blues" where you live? You can sing it if: you remember that you are God's people; you remember what you are standing for—Liberation and wholeness in our world; you remember that your "song" is needed not only in the halls of a church or for the good times but also in times of darkness and alienation when you feel as if you are in foreign and strange places.

God's song is needed by all who are wrestling with the powers and principalities of darkness. When God's songs are sung with power and conviction, lives are changed. "I" people become "we" people; the cynical and disillusioned have hope; the ritualistic dancers become involved with the real world. Biblical visions come into view, and the reign of God begins to take shape. The proud are scattered in the plans of their hearts; the mighty are cast down, and the humble exalted. Swords are beaten into plowshares. The hungry are fed; the naked are clothed; the captive are freed; the blind can see; the deaf can hear; the lame can walk; and the deceitful are exposed. Justice and mercy roll down like a mighty stream. My prayer is that we will continue to sing God's song wherever we are. Amen.

The Mind of the Insecure

Nan M. Brown

Matthew 2:1-10
**When Herod the King had heard these things, he was trou-
bled, and all Jerusalem with him. . . . And he sent them to
Bethlehem and said, Go and search diligently for the young
child; and when ye have found him, bring me word again,
that I may come and worship him also (vv. 3,8).**

The text lends itself to an exploration of and reflection on
that part of the anatomy that cyberneticists liken to the com-
puter, the brain. The text further lends itself to the study and
understanding of the mind of an irrational king who ruled

Dr. Nan M. Brown is pastor and founder of the Way of the Cross Baptist
Church, Kents Store, Virginia. She is a graduate of the Samuel Proctor
School of Theology, Virginia Union University, where she earned her D.Min.
after twenty-eight years of service in the federal government. She also
serves as CEO of the Way of the Cross Community Development
Corporation, sponsoring federally funded HIV/AIDS prevention education.

the Palestinian region at the time of our Lord's birth: Herod the Great.

Herod's reign was marked by mighty achievements. Although tyrannical, he was a great military leader and a great builder. His buildings ranged from single structures to entire cities. But Herod was a very strange combination of genius and madness, compassion and cruelty. Once during a famine in the land, he emptied his treasury to purchase food for his people. But his murderous deeds far exceeded his mercy. He had an insecure mind, a mind that was unconfident and unsure.

As Christian brothers and sisters—yea, students, preachers, pastors, teachers, and lay leaders—we need to understand what happens when an individual, like Herod, has an insatiable lust for vainglory, coupled with an insecure mind, and we also need to observe the consecrated, dedicated minds of the secure, like the wise men, as they rejoice and give glory to God.

First, the mind—that is, the faculty for thinking, reasoning, and acquiring, applying, and storing knowledge—can be either insecure or secure. That is to say, it can be unconfident and unsure, or it can have a firm belief in its own powers when coupled with the sovereign power of the Almighty.

As we examine the desperation of Herod further, we will observe an insecure mind that was first devious, then doubtful, and finally debilitating. The secure mind, on the other hand, is kind, keen, and a kindred spirit.

Herod had a mind that, though brilliant, was devious. Can you imagine how Herod's normal reasoning processes were excited by violent fury when he received the news that someone had been born who was to be king of the Jews? When Herod heard these things, he was troubled. Immediately, he began to formulate how he could rid himself of this threat, this "nuisance." Because of Herod's insecure mind, he was insanely jealous of his position and power. Now, we can very well visualize and relate our own encounters with jealous persons who have protected their positions and their power with guarded secrecy.

A seminary student who was serving a year's internship at a designated church related how frustrated he was because of the pastor's deviousness and lack of forthrightness. The pastor apparently had an insecure mind. The student intern had been assigned one specific duty: to teach the Sunday school teachers. This pastor would not allow him to preach because the intern was indeed a dynamic proclaimer of God's holy Word. On the first night of the Sunday school teachers' class, only ten teachers were present. But as the weeks progressed, the attendance increased by leaps and bounds, without any special effort on the student's part, until the entire lower level of the church was filled with teachers and non-teachers. Apparently the pastor, like Herod, became troubled when he saw these things and decided that this increase could not continue. So the pastor, the intern related later, scheduled meetings of every department of the church on the next teaching night, preventing many of the teachers from attending the teaching session. These Wednesday night meetings continued until the student completed his internship.

This example shows us what Herod's treacherousness was like. Herod, too, tolerated no rivals. Immediately following his ascension to the throne, he put to death all the members of the Sanhedrin, the ruling body of the Jews in religious and civil affairs. Herod was so insecure that he had members of his own family executed. It is easy to understand why Herod, with this kind of psychopathic mentality, was troubled about the news of the birth of the king of the Jews, Jesus the Christ. Being troubled causes individuals to react in different ways. When people are troubled, they may pace the floor in helpless, wasted motion, or they may become incapacitated. They may eat or drink too much, or, as the troubled state intensifies, they may even become frenzied, as Herod did when he received the news of the birth of a Jewish king.

There is some news that, although it is *good* news, may cause a person to focus on the negative rather than on the positive, because of that person's irrational perception or interpretation. I was visiting a hospital patient recently as a part of my role as a volunteer chaplain. The doctor had informed the patient that she would be able to go home in four days. The woman kept saying, "I hope nothing happens to keep me from going home." She had heard good news but was somehow seeing the negative rather than the positive and joyful. Such was the case with Herod. He could not interpret Jesus' birth as good news. What better news is there than the news of the birth of the Savior of the world? The insecure mind, however, is like an imperfect heartbeat. One moment it beats regularly, evenly, but the next it beats quickly, erratically. One moment the mind thinks rationally, but the next, irrationally.

Those of you who are graduating from seminary this year may serve as assistant pastors or as assistants to pastors prior to your becoming pastors. I urge you please to remember that preachers of the gospel are not excluded from feelings of insecurity. Because of this fact, we need to keep before our eyes the facts that we serve as assistants to pastors and assistant pastors and that the pastor not the assistant, is the individual who has been called by the congregation to be its shepherd. Learning can take place in both positive and negative settings. The student intern mentioned earlier learned a great deal from his frustrating experience—and so can we all—about how *not* to serve as a pastor as well as how *to* serve.

Surely Herod was troubled. He saw Jesus, who rightly should have occupied the throne, as a threat. Whenever any man, woman, or system enthrones himself/herself/itself in opposition to Jesus, a crisis develops, and there is trouble. This is why it is important that each of us assist those whom God has called. Jim Jones, who was responsible for the Guyana massacre, is a prime example of such false enthronement.

The insecure mind is not only devious, but it is also doubtful. It does not believe in anyone. Its trust level is low. The insecure mind depends far too much on its own ability. There is no room to trust an almighty God. Such a mind tries to project superiority but at the same time inwardly feels the agonizing pain of inferiority. The insecure mind, in its doubt, challenges almost every concept put before it. This mind questions for the sake of questioning, not because of the desire to learn.

It is interesting to note that not only was Herod troubled but all of Jerusalem was ill at ease. The Jews were undoubtedly aware of the king's insanity and the cruelty he inflicted when he was confronted with rivalry. They were aware of his bloodthirstiness, and they were afraid. They were troubled by their fear of this maniac. The people of Jerusalem worried, too, about what changes might take place with the coming of Messiah. They too showed doubt.

They were much like the apostle Peter with his "show-me-and-I'll-believe" attitude, displayed during his venture with Jesus in the midst of the storm when the troubled disciples saw Jesus walking on the water (Matthew 14:22-33). Jesus warned them not to be afraid. "It is I," he told them. Peter apparently was still doubtful, and said, "Lord, if it be thou, bid me to come unto thee on the water." Jesus said to Peter, "Come." Peter did, but when he saw the force of the wind, he became afraid, took his eyes off the Master, and began to sink. He cried out, "Lord, save me." Jesus, stretched forth his hand in compassion. He caught Peter and asked, "O thou of little faith, wherefore didst thou doubt?" Similarly, Jerusalem's faith was wavering.

Herod was doubtful and suspicious, so he called the chief priests and experts in religious law to inquire where Christ was born; he asked the wise men what time the star appeared in order to determine how old the child Jesus was. Surely Herod was perturbed when the theological scholars pointed out the messianic prophecies that "out of thee shall come a Governor, that shall rule my people Israel" (Matthew 2:6).

Then his mind, programmed to believe that this newborn king of the Jews would dethrone him, began to plot even further. But I perceive that now his mind moved to a third degree: debilitation. The mind was depleted of energy, depleted of nerve and strength. An insecure mind uses up its reserve on its inexorable search for security. When the mind becomes tired, the body becomes tired and limp (like the exam-time saturation point reached by students).

We are reminded of the person who sees a group talking and laughing and perceives that he or she is the subject of the conversation and laughter. We are aware of individuals who dwell on the intrigue of gaining favor, who feign worship of the Christ child but in truth only mock God. These minds are weakened by dwelling on the negative rather than the positive, always thinking the worst rather than the best. To help us to avoid debilitated minds the apostle Paul encourages us to think on things that are true, pure, just, lovely and of good report (see Philippians 4:8).

When Herod sent the wise men to Bethlehem to search diligently for the Christ child, he had no thought of worshiping him. Herod was intent on murdering him. I trust that in the Advent season we all remember whose birthday we are celebrating and give gifts to him who deserves them, worshiping him who gave us life. Herod's thoughts were those of a debilitated mind. So warped and savage was his thinking that when his death drew near, he gave orders for a group of the most distinguished citizens of Jerusalem to be arrested on trumped-up charges, imprisoned, and then killed the moment he died. Herod was aware that no one would mourn him, but he was determined that tears be shed when he died. Only a sick mind could even conceive such thoughts.

But in contrast to Herod the secure mind is kind. It exhibits love for God and fellow human beings and is considerate, compassionate, lenient, and merciful. It presses "toward the mark for the prize of the high calling of God in Christ Jesus" (Philippians 3:14). And a secure mind is keen. It is acute, quick sighted, perceptive, and enthusiastic, but it does not use its keenness to the detriment of others.

The most important characteristic of the secure mind, however, is that it is a kindred spirit because it is closely related to the spirit of God. It is a mind fashioned in the image of God, glorifying God, not itself. It does not have an insatiable desire for vainglory. This kind of mind sets its affection on things above and not on things on the earth.

It is a mind like that of the wise men: after they left Herod and saw the star again, they rejoiced with exceeding great joy; in the adoration of worship they lay at the feet of Jesus the most precious gifts they could bring; and when warned in a dream, they did not return to Herod to be part of his wickedness.

I challenge you—students, preachers, pastors, lay leaders, teachers—do not exhibit the mind of the insecure but, like Paul,

> Let this mind be in you which is in Christ Jesus: Who, being in the form of God, thought it not robbery to be equal with God: But made himself of no reputation, and took upon him the form of a servant, and was made in the likeness of men: And being found in fashion as a man, he humbled himself, and became obedient unto death, even the death of the cross (Philippians 2:5-8).

I have given myself totally to Jesus. I am sometimes troubled on every side, yet not distressed; perplexed, but not in despair; persecuted, but not forsaken; cast down, but not destroyed, always bearing within me the dying of the Lord Jesus, that the life of Jesus might be made manifest in my body (see 2 Corinthians 4:8-11). I am exceedingly happy in his service.

I challenge you further to emulate the examples of Jesus Christ and the wise men. Lay at the feet of Jesus the greatest and most noble gift one could ever give—yourselves, true servants for the Master.

Upright but *Not* Uptight

Mary Ann Allen Bellinger

Luke 13:10-17

The sabbath is the seventh day of the week on the Jewish calendar. The word *sha-bat* (sabbat) means to rest or to stop. This "rest" may have different meanings at different times for different people. And because the term "rest" could be interpreted differently by different people, it caused all kinds of questioning about what was allowable on this holy day of the Jews. Did "rest" mean to lie down and go to sleep or did it mean not to work? The rabbis listed thirty-nine different types of "work" that were prohibited on the sabbath day. Some would seem petty to us today:

—lighting a fire

Rev. Mary Ann Allen Bellinger, ordained in both Baptist and A.M.E. traditions, is currently program associate with the Office of Black Women in Church and Society at the Interdenominational Theological Center, Atlanta, Georgia. A graduate of Andover Newton Theological School, Massachusetts, she served on the Atlanta Board of Education in the late 1980s. She now serves on the staff of the First African Presbyterian Church, Lithonia, Georgia, where she is helping to write curriculum.

—clapping your hands
—jumping
—or visiting the sick

So if *I* were to interpret what "rest" meant to me, I would
have to sit in a dark room alone because when I laugh, when
I enjoy the fellowship of my sisters and brothers, I clap my
hands and jump around, and if I don't slap my thigh, I slap
someone else's!

In our story it is the sabbath, and as was his custom, Jesus
was in the synagogue teaching. As he taught, read, and
answered questions, his eyes fell on a certain woman as she
tried to make her way to the women's section of the place
of worship. She didn't notice Jesus, but I don't think she
could have seen him. She had been bent almost in half for
eighteen long years. Shoulders hunched and neck bent downward, she faced the ground like a grazing animal. Every
simple chore turned into a painful and laborious project. Even
sleep came hard. Luke the physican wrote that "she was bent
over and could not fully straighten herself" (Luke 13:11,
RSV). In other words, she was not really standing up, nor
was she helplessly lying down. She could not move about
freely, yet she was not totally immobilized. Twisted like a
human pretzel, she had learned after eighteen years not to
look up in any way at all.

Limping clumsily, head poked downward at a ridiculous
angle, she suddenly thought she heard someone speaking to
her. But, of course, after eighteen years of being ignored or
tolerated as a deformed freak, the woman did not even expect
anyone to speak to her with genuine warmth and interest.
Her world of feet and paths had not included faces with
smiles and conversation. After eighteen years of being laughed
at, tormented by the street urchins, and ignored by the self-
righteous leaders in the synagogue, the woman's first thought
was that this teacher was talking to someone else. But, finally,
she twisted her body around so she could look up. And sure
enough this man was speaking to her! Jesus called her to
him; he called her to him and placed his hands on her,
unheard-of actions for a Jewish man, particularly a rabbi.

But Jesus was unorthodox.

Remember him at the well when the woman of Samaria came to fill her waterpots in the heat of the day and he talked to her? He told her who he was. No one else in the neighborhood would talk to her, but Jesus said, "I that speak unto thee am he" (John 4:26). "I am the living water; you'll thirst no more."

Remember him at the dinner party given by Simon the Pharisee? The streetwalker came in and cried over Jesus and wiped his feet with her hair. Simon was amazed that Jesus would let a streetwalker touch him, but she was a human being in need and Jesus shut Simon up with a glance and a story.

Jesus was vividly aware of the life and love of God coming directly in touch with the need of the people.

Jesus followed the rules only insofar as they *ministered to* his brothers and sisters. He altered the rules whenever they became barriers rather than benefits to his grace. *Ministering, caring and loving* were more important to Jesus than rigid formulas, rules, habits, and customs.

Jesus called this woman to him. He reached down and placed his strong, sure, carpenter's hands on her hunched shoulders. *Jesus had to bend down!* Jesus bent himself to where she was so he could look her in the eyes. Then he told her she was loosed from her infirmity and placed his hands on her; she was immediately made straight.

The woman stretched!

She found she had been strengthened!

She could stand tall and straight!

No longer bent and twisted like an aged, gnarled tree on a windswept cliff, she assumed human-appearance!

She felt alive!

She felt human for the first time in eighteen years!

Imagine, if you will, how she must have felt to be able to stand up and look people in the face. Spontaneously she broke into an improvised doxology. She wanted to express her sense of freedom and joy! Her impromptu praises glorifying God filled the tiny synagogue. Can you see her as she realized she was able to stand up straight? She looked around at the faces of people she had never been able to see. She saw joy on some faces. She saw amazement on some. But most of all she saw *Jesus*. She lifted her arms and sang praises to God. She praised God, whom she had come to worship not knowing she would also receive her healing— healing she hadn't thought about in many years, if ever.

Ah, but make no mistake! If we are praising God and having a good time, the devil gets jealous and tries to mess things up.

The ruler of the synagogue was not touched by the woman's healing, Jesus' ministry, or the woman's joy. He was upset. He was angry. He didn't like what was happening in the synagogue on the sabbath day! He couldn't fit it into his scheme of things. All the slapping of thighs, clapping of hands, and jumping around were wrong—to him. To him the sabbath day was the day on which you walked to synagogue and passively participated in sabbath rituals. And here in his synagogue on *his* sabbath some upstart teacher was touching a woman, healing her, and allowing spontaneous songs to be lifted in praise to God! So, as Luke tells us, the synagogue ruler became indignant and told the people, "There are six days in the week for you to do all your work and also to be healed; so don't come *here* today to be *healed*. After all, it's the sabbath day!" Healing to him was work. It wasn't grace. It wasn't a gift from God. To him healing was out of place and, therefore, wrong.

And Jesus exploded!

All too often we think of Jesus as a meek and mild scaredy-cat or as some constantly courteous Hebrew Clark Kent. How do you think he drove the money changers out of the temple? With a "Please, for me, kind sir?" Don't forget that he *drove* the money changers from the temple. We need to forget we ever saw a painting that showed Jesus as a bland, blonde model for a shampoo advertisement.

Jesus exploded!

"You hypocrites!" he shouted. "You self-righteous, up-tight, rule-ridden phonies! If it's all right for you to take care of your animals, to water and feed them, on the sabbath, then I say the sabbath is a day when the work of *God* should be done as well! It's a day when the message of repentance is declared and God's salvation offered."

And, I add, if on the sabbath then there is *one, only one* time or day when salvation, healing, and repentance can take place. Jesus was raising holy havoc with the program of the synagogue. He constantly clashed with those who believed more in keeping rules than in helping people. In Christ the individual comes before the system! But here in Luke 13 we have a ruler of a synagogue who was more concerned with his petty laws than with a woman needing help. Strangely enough, this worship of systems commonly invades the church. There are many church people who are more concerned with the method of church government than with service to women and men and the worship of God! It's all too true that in the world and in the church we are constantly in peril of loving systems more than God or one another. Jesus' action in this matter makes it clear that it is *not* God's will that any human being should suffer one moment longer than absolutely necessary.

The woman who had been healed was the first to realize and understand that Jesus insisted on putting compassion ahead of cult, persons ahead of procedures. Jesus could be highly unorthodox! And being unorthordox led to tension in his ministry. But, you know, there can be a creative thrust when Jesus comes up against the status quo. Throughout Jesus' career there was turmoil. People resisted him then, and we continue to resist him today. And it will always be that way. If we know ourselves and our own blind spots, we should realize that we will resist any challenge to our pride and our will. We jump back, get uptight, and close ourselves off.

In this story recorded by Luke, we see that Jesus' confrontation brought conflict that resulted in healing and growth, not just in anger and hostility. This woman is described as having a "spirit of infirmity." But when she heard the voice of Jesus calling to her, she straightened up and immediately began to minister to those around her. What is your spirit of infirmity? Is it fear of witnessing and acknowledging Jesus as your Savior? Is it uncertainty, not knowing for sure that you are saved? Or is it a spirit of uptightness? Are you closed up within yourself, unable to reach out to others in love and welcome? I could list many possible infirmities, but one thing I'm sure we can all agree on is that every one of us has some crippling infirmity. Knowing Jesus should release us from the stooped, constricted lifestyle of seeing the footprints of our own selfishness. Through Jesus we should be aware that *God* has approached us, that God has stretched out compassionate hands to us, that God has healed us so that instead of hobbling helplessly, we can stand upright as free women and free men. We can rejoice in our new ability to stand and in our new strength. We will be like the woman in our story—we will praise God!

We don't just praise God in the sanctuary. Praising God takes many forms. Around us a world full of cripples await our hands, our help, our message of hope and salvation, and our love.

—Some are crippled by fear.
—Some are incapacitated by loneliness.
—Others are disabled by guilt.
—Many are hobbled by grief.
—Countless others are bent over by circumstances and a system that paralyzes.

In the case of the bent-over woman, the synagogue community had been content to give her handouts. They had been inclined to keep her as their "pet cripple." She enabled them to feel a little sorry and a little superior. She was to them what the neighborhood drunk, the wife beater, and child abuser are to us—they enable us to feel better than they, but we don't do much to change their lives.

Jesus went further than the rest of the synagogue community. He refused to give her aspirin, bandages, or crutches. He wanted her to be *independent* and, therefore, refused to do anything that would keep her *dependent!* He meant for her to stand as a free person, not as a pet to be fed and pitied.

Jesus calls us to be liberators, too, but some of us are afraid! The very first conflict sends us scurrying back to the safety and security of our own self-righteousness. We can't help anyone else if we are uptight ourselves. Jesus gave us the greatest gifts in the world—*life, love, liberty* and *freedom.* He gave us the freedom to touch lives with the healing word of his caring and his sacrifice.

I entitled my sermon "Upright but *Not* Uptight" because all too often when we "get religion," we figure that no one else has it like we do. We become so goody-goody that we can't praise God. And if by chance we do praise God, we want to make sure the right people are there so they can see how holy we are!

Look at this woman once again. When Jesus called her, she went forward and received healing. When she was healed, she didn't hold onto her joy selfishly but immediately began to minister to those around her in the synagogue. Praise God! She sang! Praise God! She encouraged!

What did you do when God did something in *your* life? Do you say you don't remember because it's been so long? Every single day God does something special just for you. Do you feel that you have had a relationship with God for so long that you are ashamed to admit that you aren't sure you still have what you once thought you had?

This woman had been bent over double for eighteen years. For eighteen years she had been attending worship services. She had the appearance of faith, but she had not accepted the power of God to make a change in her life. She accepted her condition because she didn't think she could be any other way. But one day she heard the voice of Jesus and everything changed!

And today I, a sinner saved by grace, by God's grace, called by God to preach the Word, can stand here before you and offer you Jesus: Savior, Counselor, Comforter. And when you get to know him for yourself, you, too, are given the privilege, the right, and the joy of offering him to others!

But you must hear Jesus first. You must hear him say to you, "Be loosed from your infirmities." Whatever your infirmity may be, only Jesus can loose you from it. If it's a bad attitude, rolling your eyes, hunching your shoulders, looking bored, poking out your lips, whispering about folks, only Jesus can loose you! If it's a big ego, "Mr. Know-it-all" or "Miss Can't-tell-me-a-thing," let Jesus loose you!

You check yourself—I don't know you well enough to do that for you—but God knows all about you and you can't fool God. So check yourself, not your neighbor, spouse, or friend.

When Jesus comes in, uptightness goes out.

When you are loosed from your infirmities, you are free. Praise God!

Studying War Some More

Sharon E. Williams

War has always been an enterprise to be hated, avoided, and shunned. It does not suit the Christian personality. Christ encourages us to be meek, humble, and lowly, to be peace-making and merciful. We are supposed to be shining lights in a dark world. War is just not our thing. We are not made for war and strife. We are not made for violence. We are made for the kingdom of God. We are made for that realm of divine blessing where peace and goodwill abound for all.

But even the kingdom suffers violence. Jesus pointed out that from the time John the Baptist began preaching the

Sharon E. Williams accepted God's call to the ministry after many years as an office worker in government, social services, and private industry. She earned a Master of Divinity degree from Union Theological Seminary, New York City. She interned at the Abyssinian Baptist Church and later served as Minister of Christian education at Union Baptist Church in New York City, where her work included ministry in prisons, hospitals, denominational schools, and seminaries, as well as work in political action campaigns. Presently she is pastor of the Church of the Redeemer, Brooklyn, New York.

kingdom, two things happened: the kingdom *suffered* violence, and the violent *took* the kingdom by force (see Matthew 11:12).

We know in our own time that peace is broken by violence—even in the Christian journey. We are not exempt from rape, mugging, or murder. Our peace with God, family and one another is taken from us by violence. I learned a while ago that a woman died on a subway platform in New York City during the Fourth of July weekend. Someone threw a cherry bomb at her to distract her and then snatched her purse. She was so frightened that she had a heart attack and died. Suddenly came an unexpected encounter with meanness and violence; her peace was snatched from her, and she died.

Earlier this year our church funeralized a mother and two small children who had been brutally murdered in their own home. An older child in the family was arrested for the crime: a family's peace and joy were snatched away by violence. Unity and love were replaced by separation and grief.

From out of nowhere violence comes to assault the kingdom. From out of nowhere—attack! From behind masked faces—violence and destruction! From the skies and from under the earth—suffering and death. The kingdom suffers. The kingdom is taken.

It does not seem fair of God to create us for peace and love and then allow all this violence. It is not fair for the violent to be allowed to take the kingdom from us. Is God's kingdom that fragile and vulnerable? Is it okay for us—the meek and lowly—to take up armaments against this violence, at least for our own safety, in a violent world?

> For though we live in the world we are not carrying on a worldly war, for the weapons of our warfare are not worldly but have divine power to destroy strongholds. We destroy arguments and every proud obstacle to the knowledge of God, and take every thought captive to obey Christ . . . (2 Corinthians 10:3-5, RSV).

These few verses speak to us in our day of sudden massacres. These verses speak to every instance of assault, robbery, burglary, torture, abuse, war, strife, and violence. These verses speak to all manner of evildoing.

Thus saith the Lord: We are made for peace *and* war.

Jesus *does* say in Matthew 5: "Blessed are the peacemakers: for they shall be called the children of God." But he *also* says in Matthew 10: "Think not that I am come to bring peace on earth: I came not to bring peace, but a sword." Jesus continues this teaching by showing us those very things of the flesh, of the world, *against which* he has set us: father, mother, household—even ourselves. We are set against all things of the world that we love more than Christ.

Jesus sent us to war, but not against one another. We are at war with the violence and evil which assault or threaten or diminish the kingdom. We are at war with anything that comes between God and the world God so loved that he gave his only Son to die for it. Paul says it better in Ephesians 6: "For we wrestle not against flesh and blood, but against principalities, against powers. . . ." We wrestle against rulers of darkness. We are at war with spiritual wickedness.

There is a war going on, and we are involved in it. It is not the world's war of violence. It is *our* war. The tricky and even dangerous thing about our war is to make sure we fight *our* war and not *their* war. Their war is a war against us. Their war is a war of violence. Their war is devoted to total destruction. Their war is the way of the world.

But our war is different. Our war is not against people. Our war is against the darkness and spiritual wickedness *in them*. Our war is not a war of violence. Our war is a war of salvation and deliverance. Our war is not devoted to the destruction of the enemy but rather to new life for the enemy— a life free from violence. This war—our war—is the way of the Spirit. Remember these things: We are made for peace *and* war. But we must always be clear as to whose war we are fighting.

Thus saith the Lord: The weapons of our warfare are mighty *through God*.

We, the lovers of peace, are the only ones who can truly say that God is on our side. Because we wrestle not against flesh and blood, God is on our side. It is not God's will that the world (that is, flesh and blood) be destroyed. God's will is that the world be redeemed, saved, and brought to righteousness. God is *not* against the wicked, God is against *wickedness*. As long as we war against wickedness (and not against the wicked), God and we will be on the same side.

It is necessary that we remain clearheaded about *who* the enemy is. Jesus said, "Love your enemy." Here he was talking about the *person* who perpetrates evil. An attack (whether offensive *or* defensive) against *persons* is not what our war is about! I repeat: The enemies we fight are powers, principalities, rulers of darkness, and spiritual wickedness. Our weapons are to be only those effective against our *real* enemies. Against spiritual enemies *we must use spiritual weapons*!

We know there are many spirits. However, we also know that the most powerful and reliable weapons are spiritual weapons, which come from God. Forgiveness is stronger than revenge. Gentleness is more powerful than brutishness. Patience wins over haste, self-control and temperance over excess, caring over covetousness, upbuilding over jealousy, truth over lies, lowliness over self-exaltation.

Yes, it is *our* war, but it is mighty and victorious through God. At the height of a dangerous and life-threatening battle, our surrender to the shaping of the Holy Ghost is our guarantee of victory. Holy weapons tear down the stronghold of the enemy. God's weapons draw our enemies out of their hiding places. The Holy Ghost captures the souls of evildoers by cutting off their supply lines and tearing down the strongholds of darkness, fleshliness, spiritual ignorance, and even sin itself.

Remember this: God can do these things, and we can do them only through God.

Thus saith the Lord: In every war there are casualties. If you plan to fight, you have to face the possibility of getting hurt or even killed. That's what the enemy is about—wounding, maiming, and killing. So what you need is some protection. You need something that will keep the weapons of the enemy from being effective against you. You need something to protect you against bombs and bullets, knives and clubs. You need something to protect you from sickness and ill health.

You need something to keep you from getting demoralized and discouraged. In wartime you need some armor.

But you need the right kind of armor. In one kind of war you need one kind of armor. In another kind of war you need another kind of armor. In spiritual warfare you need some spiritual armor. In God's war you need God's armor—all that you can get. You need the whole armor of God not so that you can fight the war, but so that you can withstand the war. The Holy Ghost gives you your weapons (you know, the fruits of the Spirit—peace, love, longsuffering, and so on). But Jesus gives you your armor.

Jesus girds your loins with the clean white linen of truth. Wrapped all around and about you is Jesus—the Word, the Truth, the Life. So when you find yourself in the midst of battle, and you believe your cause is lost—when you begin to doubt that you are on the side of truth, love, and justice—then you can just look at yourself in your clean white loincloth and declare, as Job declared: "I know that my Redeemer liveth." When you think you may go under, you can claim as Job claimed: ". . . though after my skin worms destroy this body, yet in my flesh shall I see God." You can stand and *with*stand when you have the Way, the Truth, and the Life.

In the war Jesus also issues the regulation breastplate: the breastplate of righteousness. War, you see, is nasty business. Even the sincerest heart is vulnerable to the weaponry of the world. In war your heart can be pierced with corruption. In war your heart can grow tired of beating against the rhythm and pulse of the world. In war it is hard to *stay* righteous. So Jesus has given you all the righteousness you need in the righteousness of the cross. No longer do you have to *prove* your worth, your value, your righteousness. You don't have to *earn* your way to the warrior's reward. In this battle you have righteousness for your very breastplate. It's strapped right on the front of you for everyone else to see—including yourself.

And as you go into battle, your feet are wearing a new pair of shoes. They have been shaped and molded for the battle, so that you are prepared for the ordeal to come. Your special "marching boots" are called the gospel of Peace. You walk in peace. You run in peace. You bring peace with you. You take peace wherever you go. Through the rockets' red glare—peace. Bombs bursting in air—peace. There's peace through the night. There's peace through the fight. Forget about the flag. Just keep your boots polished and shiny.

Above all, let's be shielded with faith: the substance of things hoped for in wartime, the evidence of victory not yet seen, the proof that the battle is won and the victory is God's. With faith we are able to put out the darts of fire with which the wicked surround us and threaten us. In the fiery furnace we have faith. In the devouring flames we have faith. Faith brings cool waters. Faith quenches the thirst. Faith brings the washing, cleansing, purifying shower in which nothing can burn.

Above all is faith! We can do nothing without it! We can do anything with it!

But, you know, I still feel a little underdressed. I can't resist putting on one extra piece. You see, Jesus puts out this fantastic helmet. It took him three whole days to make it up just for me. He began forging the metal one Friday in the scorching noonday sun. And he didn't finish it until Sunday morning in the cool darkness of a rich man's tomb. When the stone was rolled away, out came Jesus, carrying my helmet of salvation.

I just can't go out into battle with my head uncovered. Since 95 percent of a person's body heat goes out through an uncovered head, I'm going into battle with my head covered with salvation.

And while Jesus was working on my helmet, he fashioned a sword, which he called the Holy Ghost. He didn't issue it with the helmet. That sword came special delivery to a crowded upper room some fifty days later. The sword came just as he had promised. I can't go to war without my sword.

And I can't go to war without the Word. I've got my Bible, and I've got my helmet. I've got some faith, and my new shoes feel good on my feet. My breastplate is strapped on and my loins are girded round about.

I'm waging war by forgiving all enemies.
I'm waging war by practicing gentleness.
I'm waging war by giving up jealousy and backbiting.
I'm waging war by walking in a meek and lowly way.
I'm waging war by telling the truth, even when I am threatened by violent liars.
I'm waging war by bringing peace.
I'm waging war by feeding the hungry.
I'm waging war by supplying the poor with what they need.
I'm waging war by healing the sick.
I'm waging war by having patience and reconciliation.
I'm waging war by having a contrite and broken spirit.
I'm waging war by a will surrendered to God.
I'm waging war.

A Prescription for Humility

Marjorie Leeper Booker

Have this mind among yourselves, which is yours in Christ Jesus, who, though he was in the form of God, did not count equality with God a thing to be grasped, but emptied himself, taking the form of a servant, being born in the likeness of men. And being found in human form he humbled himself and became obedient unto death, even death on a cross. Therefore God has highly exalted him and bestowed on him the name which is above every name . . . (Philippians 2:5-9, RSV).

Paul, writing to the church at Philippi, pleaded for unity among the members. He encouraged them to follow the example of Christ in seeking togetherness. He told them that

Rev. Marjorie Leeper Booker has served as pastor of Koinonia Christian Church (Independent) of Richmond, Virginia, for the past twenty-five years. Her husband has served during this time as her associate pastor. She is a graduate of the Virginia Commonwealth College and of the Samuel Proctor School of Theology, Virginia Union University. A mother and grandmother, she is also active in the Richmond community.

their attitudes toward the church and life would be meaningful and peaceful if they would but act as Christ. Paul then gave them a prescription for acquiring humility. Many of us today may find the need for this same prescription when we examine our lives.

The First Ingredient: The Emptying of Self

Paul made it known that Jesus emptied himself of the attitude of *"my* right." Jesus did not believe equality with God was something to be grasped. For a higher gain and a greater glory, he could relinquish his position as being one with God. Jesus emptied himself of all feelings of *his* right to be or *his* right to do. He became subordinate to God. Even though from the very beginning the position at God's right hand was rightfully his, Jesus was able to give it up. He did not become resentful when conditions made it necessary for him to relinquish that claim for the good of humankind.

Often we hold positions in high places and refuse to step down when conditions would best be served if we did. Christ was never concerned with making a name for himself; he was concerned with doing the will of God. His mission was to bridge the gap between persons and God.

Most of us labor hard and spend much time and energy gaining a social reputation for ourselves. Our ultimate aim is to be accepted, and often in accomplishing this, we make the sky the limit. Too often, we are forced to wear masks: true feelings, frustrations, and weaknesses are hidden, and who we are as real persons is seldom seen or allowed to be seen. Young people, adults, and old folks all wear masks at one time or another. It was the little children whom Christ used to illustrate the right attitudes that will allow us to enter into heaven, for a child will always be himself or herself, with a mind unpolluted by the selfishness and social seeking of the world.

Why is a social reputation important to us? No matter how much we say we want to please God, we direct our attention to pleasing people. When we have gained society's approval, we then develop a sense of security, and pleasing God becomes secondary. This kind of attitude eventually leads to our destruction. If we would look back into history, we might find that everyone who ever did anything meaningful and who did things God's way was rejected by society and in many instances was left standing alone. Those who have the mind of Jesus are seldom popular with the majority. Paul himself was counted with the minority. Jesus was rejected and many times stood alone.

Many of us today can boast of academic achievements, social advancements, political accomplishments, secure jobs, and the like. Quite often such achievements take first place in our lives. Salvation then comes through social status.

Family names may become a means of salvation. If one is connected with the right family, then salvation is assured and society shuts its eyes to whatever wrong is being done, excusing it because of who is doing it. When a poor man drinks, he is classed as a drunkard; when a rich man drinks, he is viewed as easing his tension, calming his nerves. When the poor choose not to attend church, they are seen as sinners; when the affluent choose not to go, they are viewed as being just too busy. The measure by which we judge others is often predicated on who is doing something rather than on what is being done.

We must empty ourselves of all that may separate us from God. To empty ourselves may mean that prejudice and superior attitudes must take flight. We cannot allow prejudice and superior attitudes to control our actions. Christ was not partial. All were the same in his sight. He helped the poor and the rich, the mighty and the small, and the strong and the weak. We need to remember this when dealing with our sisters and brothers in Christ, for quite often color, race, creed, and the like, will condition our actions.

To empty ourselves may mean that we must let go of our egos. To be able to do this will be the ultimate act of self-denial, for many of us are puffed up with foolish pride. Egotism has been a problem for people from the very beginning of creation. Pride would not allow Adam and Eve to empty themselves, and it resulted in their (and our) competing with God. If we are not careful, we will find ourselves playing God, overly self-reliant and turning from God to do things our way. This kind of attitude always ends in disaster. It causes us to put our welfare before that of others. Paul certainly admonished the Christians at Philippi to look after their own interests—and we all should do that—but never at the expense of others (Philippians 2:4). Selfish pride, empty boasting, and seeking one's own interest to the exclusion of others, are all common symptoms of selfishness, a disease that attacks human beings. Our egos prevent us from seeing the other side of the coin, the other person's point of view. We believe that our way must prevail if peace is to be maintained. This kind of attitude is not of Christ—for Christ emptied himself of all thoughts of self above others.

The Second Ingredient: Acquiring the Mind of Christ

Christ humbled himself, taking the form of a servant. A servant serves. Jesus said that if anyone would be great, let him or her become a servant. Not only did Jesus say this, but he demonstrated it when he washed the disciples' feet and, most importantly, when he left his heavenly throne to come into a world of woe. He stated that he came to serve, not to be served. In our society the great are served. In Christian discipleship the great must do the serving. This usually presents a problem in the church when those in authority insist on being served and catered to instead of serving. Many church leaders reserve special privileges for themselves and refuse to do menial tasks because of their positions. Some believe that to perform these menial tasks is degrading and below their dignity. If the church of God is to progress, it must rid itself of such an attitude and take on the attitude of Christ.

(The attitude of wanting to be served also presents problems in the home and in our city, state, and national government. Many of our leaders do little serving; they expect much service from those whom they should be serving. Too often people holding public jobs forget that they are servants and often become impatient and annoyed with those whom they are supposed to serve.)

"What is man?" Job asked (see Job 38; 40:4). Job discovered that humankind was nothing when he compared it to God's sovereignty. Humankind was created by God, the Creator. The created are never greater than the Creator. When people realize this, humbleness will come more easily. To be humble is to realize a higher and greater power than oneself. Without God, nothing is lasting, for all that we can accomplish will soon perish. God gives all things and God takes away at will. Only those things done for Christ will last. Material wealth will fade away, and worldly fame and glory will one day vanish. Even a good name will eventually fade into history. Only God and God's love are eternal.

Being found in human form, Jesus knew what it was to be human. There is nothing that humankind can experience that Christ did not experience. He suffered pain, sorrow, anguish, misgivings, disappointments, and rejection. He experienced love and he witnessed hatred. In his humanity, he drew closer to God. All this is the mind of Christ to be acquired.

The Third Ingredient: Obedience

Jesus was obedient. It is hard for us to obey because of our rebellious nature. Most of us are willing to obey when we recognize our helpless state. Nevertheless, how many of us (and how often do we) recognize the fact that we are helpless without the grace of God? Christ became helpless in order to help us. Even in the face of opposition and persecution, he did not turn aside but remained obedient, even unto death on the cross. He died the death of a criminal, yet he was without sin.

It is easy to obey when all is going well, but when opposition and persecution result from our obedience, we may choose not to obey, and then the law of self-preservation takes over. That is, we usually obey when it best serves our interests, and in many instances we find ourselves selling out to avoid persecution when it comes. But Jesus did not sell out. He remained obedient. When the forces of his day rose against him, he remained faithful. He believed God and accepted the plan obediently. He did not think of his own interest but looked beyond the stigma and pain of the cross to deliverance. He knew it was necessary for him to go to the cross, but he looked beyond the necessity of the cross and deemed it a joy and a privilege to obey God. We need a faith like that of Christ, a faith that would cause us to sing the words of William H. Bathurst:

> O for a faith that will not shrink
> Tho' pressed by ev'ry foe.
> That will not tremble on the brink
> Of any earthly woe.

Obedience, then, comes through faith. When we believe in something or someone, obedience will not come hard. The problem comes when our lips profess what our hearts deny. Jesus was obedient, even to death on the cross. His obedience redeemed you and me from the death of sin. It brought us into a right relationship with God. His death on the cross represents the height of obedience and shows us the extent of God's love.

Conclusion

We have discussed the three ingredients that are required for true humility as set forth by Jesus Christ: the emptying of self, humility, and true obedience. Paul set forth these virtues, which Jesus had portrayed in his saving act. With this prescription one can acquire the mind of Christ.

How will the mind of Christ benefit us? With the mind of Christ we will be able to live the life we talk about. We will be able to overcome the temptation to glorify and gratify ourselves. We will be able to hear the cries of the needy and the deprived and be sensitive to their needs. We will be able to deny ourselves and put the interest of others before our own. We will be able to pick up our crosses daily and follow Christ. We will be able to obey God and do God's will, saying, like Jesus, "Not my will but thine be done." With the mind of Christ we will be able to rise up and speak out against injustice, wherever and whenever it may be found. With the mind of Christ we will be able to look at all God's children as sisters and brothers in Christ. We will be able to play together, grow together, live together, love together, and serve God together.

One day, God spoke to my sin-stained soul. On that day I emptied myself of all my false pride and answered the call. I met with much opposition and suffered persecution, but the grace of God has sustained me and I have obeyed. It pays to obey God. Israel realized this, for when it obeyed, it prospered, and when it disobeyed, it suffered hardships. Enoch walked with God and was taken up. Abraham obeyed God and because of his faithfulness became the father of many nations. Jesus obeyed God and was exalted. Paul says that because of the mind that Christ had, God exalted him and gave him a name above all names.

The same reward is promised to you and me. If we but put on the mind of Christ, we too shall be exalted. Empty yourself, humble yourself, and obey God. You will be victorious, and peace will reign in your life.

The Blessings and Burdens of the Divinely Chosen

Clara Mills

Acts 9:15-22

Throughout the pages of the Bible, we see that God carefully selected persons to perform particular tasks and/or services. These persons spanned the spectrum in terms of the qualities and types of personality, social involvement, academic orientation, and accomplishments. Some of these persons who were carefully selected by God were ordinary in their accomplishments and approaches toward life, while others had made extraordinarily significant contributions in many areas. Many of these persons possessed enormous natural gifts and abilities and recognized these as resources

Rev. Clara Mills is a graduate of Virginia Commonwealth University, with an M.Div. from the Samuel Proctor School of Theology, Virginia Union University, both in Richmond. She has done advanced work in clinical pastoral studies and served as consultant in relationships and communication and as director of holistic ministries in the San Francisco area. She served recently as associate secretary in the Southern California Conference of the United Church of Christ.

and utilized them effectively. Others viewed themselves as worthless, inferior, and incompetent because they bore certain physical and/or emotional handicaps. Some of these persons who constituted the ranks of the "divinely chosen" were labeled as physically attractive and pleasant to behold, while others were lacking in those physical characteristics that would move them beyond the category of the "plain and simple." Many of these "divinely chosen" persons lived good and righteous lives prior to their divine calling, while others exhibited a great deal of insensitivity and lack of concern for the rights and welfare of others.

There is nothing typical about those who were divinely chosen that gained for them this special selection; they were as different in their makeup, as varying in their abilities and gifts, as every other human being. Even the tasks and services for which these persons were chosen were of varying types. The apostle Paul, in one of his letters to the Christians in Corinth, delineates this diversity. Paul in 1 Corinthians 12:5-10 wrote:

> Now there are differences of administrations, but the same Lord. And there are diversities of operations, but it is the same God which worketh all in all. But the manifestation of the Spirit is given to every man to profit withal. For to one is given by the Spirit the word of wisdom; to another the word of knowledge by the same Spirit; to another faith by the same Spirit; to another the gifts of healing by the same Spirit; to another the working of miracles; to another prophecy; to another discerning of spirits; to another diverse kinds of tongues; to another the interpretation of tongues
> . . . .

Those who were divinely chosen were not chosen because they were special; rather, they became special because they were divinely chosen.

The divinely chosen enter into a very strange and peculiar world—a world in which they become recipients of many rich blessings and at the same time victims of untold burdens, burdens which at times seem to sap every ounce of their strength and vitality. There are times when the divinely chosen strut with pride and dignity because of the presence and power of God's Holy Spirit, which is keenly felt and profoundly projected. And yet there are times when these same divinely chosen persons seem to carry the very weight of the world on their shoulders. There are times when "the windows of heaven" seem to pour out rich, invigorating blessings, when the divinely chosen feel productive and appreciated and are able to measure the results of their labors by the many lives that have been drastically changed. And there are times when the vision of these same divinely chosen persons is clouded by the many criticisms and scandals that at times are overwhelmingly pronounced on them.

The divinely chosen, like everyone else, have high days and low days. Though motivated and sustained by the same Holy Spirit, these divinely chosen struggle to allow their wills and spirits to become immersed in the Spirit of God. Whether preacher, teacher, philanthropist, philosopher, healer, helper, or administrator, all divinely chosen persons must live from one experience to the next, never sure of the nature or outcome of any experience, only confident of the presence of God and the fact that "all things work together for good to them that love God, to them who are called according to his purpose" (Romans 8:28).

The blessings and burdens of the divinely chosen.

Let us utilize the apostle Paul as a scriptural and historical reference and resource for this message. In the ninth chapter of the book of Acts, we encounter Paul, then referred to as Saul, as he was traveling on a certain Damascus road, on his way to persecute those who were following the teachings and practices of Jesus of Nazareth, the Christ.

This man Saul was the product of many cultural and religious influences. A Roman citizen, well educated in the Graeco-Roman traditions, he grew to become an avid supporter and defender of the Roman government. He was also a Jew, a very proud Jew, well versed in the Judaic scriptures and a strict adherent to the teachings and practices of the Judaic faith. In Paul's letter to the Christians in Philippi he wrote concerning this phase in his life:

> If anyone thinks he may have confidence in the flesh, I more so: circumcised on the eighth day of the stock of Israel, of the tribe of

Benjamin, a Hebrew of Hebrews; . . . concerning zeal, persecuting
the church; concerning the righteousness which is in the law,
blameless (Philippians 3:4-6, paraphrased).

Saul was no ordinary or average person. He approached life
with a greater than average intensity, seriousness, and commitment to himself, to the Roman government, and to the
Judaic faith.

While traveling to Damascus, Saul encountered the spiritual presence of Jesus of Nazareth, the resurrected Lord.
According to the story, a light shone from heaven, shone
around Saul; he fell to the ground and heard a voice saying,
"Saul, Saul, why are you persecuting me?" Imagine the star-
tling impact this initial experience must have had on Saul.
No doubt he was filled with fear and astonishment. One of
the interesting qualities about God is that God always reaches
us where we are. It was because of the depth of Saul's personality and the extraordinariness of his character that his
initial encounter with the Eternal was so breathtakingly pro-
found.

Saul was told to go into the city of Damascus, where he
would be told what he would have to do. "Trembling and
astonished, he arose from the ground, opened his eyes only
to discover that his sight was gone. He was then led by the
hand, and brought into Damascus" (Acts 9:6-8, paraphrased).

There was a man named Ananias, a disciple of Jesus the
Christ, who received a vision from the Lord. In this vision
Ananias was told to go to Saul and lay hands on him so that
Saul might receive his sight and be filled with God's Holy
Spirit.

Isn't it interesting how the Lord manages to place us in
the most uncomfortable situations, with those persons who
bring out all the fears and anxieties that often lie buried deep
within us?

Ananias was scared stiff! Although he probably on previous
occasions had responded unreservedly to God's beckoning,
this time Ananias hesitated. He even wondered, no doubt,
whether God was sure of the task to which God called him.
"Lord," Ananias responded, "I have heard from many about

this man and how much harm he has done to your saints in Jerusalem." But the word of God yet came to Ananias: "Go, for he is a chosen vessel of mine, to bear my name before the Gentiles, kings, and the children of Israel, for I will show him how many things he must suffer for my name's sake."

The blessings and burdens of the divinely chosen.

Let us consider first the burdens experienced by the divinely chosen. One such burden grows out of the tension that exists between the special character implied from being *chosen* and the realization that as a mere vessel, there is no self-value or self-worth apart from the One who has made the selection. The egos of the divinely chosen are in constant tension with the realization that they are *nothing apart from and independent of God*. The divinely chosen live with the indisputable truth that every gift possessed, every miracle wrought, every seed sown, every soul saved occurs only because of the tremendous power of the eternal Spirit that dwells within them. The preacher preaches, and souls are saved. The teacher teaches, and learning and growth take place. The philanthropist gives resources, and vital improvements are made possible. The physician administers the proper care and treatment, and healing occurs. Yet they all realize that their resources are given by God and that the results are made possible because of the blessings of God. Beatrice Brown expressed this with tremendous clarity when she wrote, "Without God, I can do nothing; without God I would fail; without God my life would be rugged, like a ship without a sail."

Yet another burden experienced by the divinely chosen is that they must live with the constant skepticism of others. Following Saul's encounter with the resurrected Lord, in spite of his strivings on behalf of the ministry of Jesus Christ and in spite of the fruits of his labors, there were those who doubted his sincerity and were distrustful of his intentions.

There will always be people who will be skeptical of the divinely chosen because they "knew them when. . . ." Skepticism, however, must be neither ignored nor confronted but addressed through sincerity and commitment that will eventually command attention.

The divinely chosen also live with the burden of continuously wrestling with the Adversary. The divinely chosen must never fool themselves into thinking that because one battle has been won, the war is over, for the Christian life (which is no different in this sense from life itself) is a series of battles. It is because of this continuous wrestling with the forces of evil that the divinely chosen must always be in the process of spiritually preparing themselves to cope and deal effectively with the insurmountable pressures of each new experience, always approaching life cautiously.

The tendency, when we find ourselves in difficult situations, is to blame ourselves. We often nag ourselves with the question "What have I done?" Often we have not done a thing. Many of the negative experiences we encounter come because we are at a particular point in time and space. At other times we encounter negative experiences because of what we represent.

However, in spite of the burdens encountered by the divinely chosen, they experience the blessed realization that the God who "carefully selects" them also carefully watches over them. Let's look now at some of these blessings.

At times the pressures around the divinely chosen will be of so great a magnitude that the presence of God seems more an idea than a reality. We would do well to remember that God is wherever we are. In our moments of deepest sorrow, God is there! In our moments of decision and uncertainty, God is there! Through the prophet Isaiah God assured the people of Israel of his abiding presence, and these assuring words are for us even today:

> You whom I have taken from the ends of the earth, and called from its farthest regions, and said to you "You are my servant, I have chosen you and have not cast you away"; fear not, I am with you; be not dismayed, for I am your God. I will strengthen you, yes, I will help you, I will uphold you with my righteous hand (Isaiah 41:9-10, paraphrased).

The divinely chosen are also blessed with a spirit that, though crushed, will never die; a spirit that has no fear of the powers of men and women but one that exudes confidence and self-assurance, confounding the wicked; a spirit that is strenghtened and sustained because of the hope in the promises of God. What are some of these promises? One is the promise of God's abiding presence expressed by Jesus Christ to his disciples on the eve of his ascension—"And be assured, I am with you always, to the end of time" (Matthew 28:20, NEB). Another is the promise of God's peace, a perfect peace which passeth all human understanding; yet another is the promise of God's Holy Spirit, who empowers and enables.

Further, the divinely chosen are blessed with the undying support of a faithful few who will attest to the impact of the labors of the chosen. I am reminded of the life and ministry of my grandmother, the Reverend Ethel Virginia Tatnall. She was indeed a divinely chosen vessel. Granny, in terms of physical stature, was a small woman, standing about 4 feet, 11 inches tall; but in terms of the impact of her life and ministry on the lives of others, she was a giant of a woman. She was much like the apostle Paul in that she approached life with a greater-than-average intensity. She was a rare breed in terms of her natural gifts and abilities, but, more important, in terms of the extent to which she utilized her gifts to the glory of God. A magnificent preacher, she, indeed, effectively combined the intellectual and emotional components in sermonic preparation and delivery.

Many persons were impressed and affected by Granny's counseling, teaching, and preaching ministry, which spanned sixty years.

As Granny's life approached its concluding pages, as her eyesight grew dim, as her joints stiffened and caused her mobility to decrease, as the vividness and sharpness of her mental faculties grew dim, the attention received from the countless persons touched by her life and ministry diminished. There were just a faithful few who continued to be supportive, who could not forget—nor would they let her forget—the impact of her life and ministry on their lives. It was these faithful few who gave Granny the joy and confidence she so desperately needed during the last days of her life.

The blessings and burdens of the divinely chosen may be summed up in the words of Acts 9:15-16:

But the Lord said to him [Ananias], Go thy way: for he [Saul] is a *chosen vessel unto me*, to bear my name before the Gentiles, and kings, and the children of Israel: for I will shew him how great things he must suffer for my name's sake   (Acts 9:15-16, emphasis added).

Letting Go

Beverly J. Shamana

Isaiah 43:15-21
**"Remember not the former things, nor consider the things
of old. Behold, I am doing a new thing; now it springs forth,
do you not perceive it?" (Isaiah 43:18-19, RSV).**

There is something unsettling about being told to forget
the past. We are startled, and maybe even repelled, by the
scriptural phrase "Consider [not] the things of old." There
is, without a doubt, something within us that enshrines the
past and fears the future. The prophet delivered these timely
words to a people who clung desperately to the way life used
to be. Let us then consider these words so that we may
discover what it means to "remember not."

That ragged, scraggly band of exiles known to us as the

Bishop Beverly J. Shamana presides over the Northern California/Nevada
Conference of the United Methodist Church, with offices in West Sacramento,
California. A graduate of Garrett-Evangelical Theological Seminary in Evanston,
Illinois, she has served numerous pastorates, including the First Methodist Church
of Inglewood, California, and on various commissions of the United Methodist
Church, such as the Status and Role of Women.

children of Israel had a debt to collect from Egypt, a score to settle with the past, and collect they would—with interest! You can almost hear them:

"I was deprived of my youth in Egypt."

"All my children were born slaves to Pharaoh."

"Egypt . . . that's where my husband died. . . ."

"My soul was scarred in slavery."

"Egypt . . . death . . . loss. . . ."

Over and over the prophet tried to counter their despair and discontent. "See what God has done. You have not been deserted. You have been saved. You did not die; you were delivered. You're here. Praise God!"

It's tough to throw our old baggage overboard even when it's useless. How do we let go of our slavery? Very slowly, says the voice of one crying in the wilderness. "Dis-remembering" our captivity is hard work. It is painful to forget our bondage and live our freedom. It is doubly painful when we have leftover debts to collect from our subjugation.

Though no longer captives, the people of Israel held to a slave mentality. "I can't do anything about the future; someone else controls my life. What will the master think? What will the pharaoh do?" How tenaciously we cling to patterns, relationships, and ways of thinking about the world that served another time, another situation!

A friend recently told me how she'd been urging her brother and his wife to see Europe. Thinking this to be the trip of a lifetime, she excitedly helped plan their itinerary. "You must see this cathedral—and don't forget that museum." "Why don't you come with us?" he said with a wry grin one evening. "Who me?" she said, startled." Why I can't leave the children." Later she related the incident to her daughter. "Mother, you must be kidding. Are you talking about my brother and sister? sixteen and nineteen years old? Are these the children you can't leave for one week — for a trip of a lifetime?" Click. Her freedom had sneaked up on her. Like the Israelites, the reasons, the patterns, the relationships that had appropriately served her in the past, and, indeed, had assured her survival, had also chained her to the past.

O freedom. O freedom. O freedom over me.

Oh, what a clarion call rings out to us from the depth of this spiritual! What a clear and persistent call beckons us from the depths of our people, who knew what it meant to be deprived of their youth in slavery, to bear their children in slavery, to lose their husbands in slavery, to scar their souls in slavery. But the indomitable human and divine alliance authored by God will not stay captive, will not be fettered.

> And before I'd be a slave
> I'd be buried in my grave;
> And go home to my Lord and be free.

Before I'd be captive and chained, defined by anything less than God's boundless freedom, I'd go home to my Lord . . . and be free!

And yet there's more to this business of moving forward than is apparent at first glance. Even deeper than "dis-re-membering" our comfortable and treasured survival tactics is the knowledge that Isaiah calls us to forgive the past. Yes, forgive the past. The prayer of Jesus says, "Forgive us our debts," i.e., forgive us our past, even as we forgive the debts the past owes us. "Remember not the former things, nor consider the things of old. Behold, I am doing a new thing; now it springs forth, do you not perceive it?"

The Scripture promises that as you begin to let go of the past, God will create a new thing in your midst, and it will be even better than it was before. And you thought parting the Red Sea was something! Wait till you see rivers in the desert! More glorious than before — and water in the wil-derness! Even the animals will rejoice in a desert that is transformed, where all creatures will praise their Maker.

I ask you, what new things could God create in you and through you if you could give wings to old business, bless the past, say a prayer over it, and release it to God? You will find that as you forgive those IOUs, hurts, injustices, and rejections of the past, you will be paid larger reparations than you could have imagined: more than seventy times seven, in grace-filled ways.

How shall we move into God's future without trepidation? One poet aptly describes our fear and fascination this way:

> "Come to the edge," he said.
> They said: "We are afraid."
> "Come to the edge," he said.
> They came.
> He pushed them . . . and they flew.

Moving forward from today can feel like going to the edge. But we can fly. And what refreshing sustenance God provides while we try our wings! Rivers are supplied in the desert and water in the wilderness.

What is it we are called to forgive? What debt do we hold, still waiting to collect interest? We carry around a heavy load of expectations that come from "out there": "They say . . ." and "But you promised." No matter what our age or circumstance, we all have a "But you promised" list.

—But you promised that my parents would be perfect, that they would never let me down. *You owe me!*

—But you promised that if I majored in liberal arts, I would always have a job; you said it was good for girls. *You owe me!*

—But you promised that my children would appreciate the sacrifices I made, that they would repay me by looking after me in my old age. At least they would live nearby. *You owe me!*

—But you promised that if I didn't abuse my body with chemicals and drugs, if I exercised and ate properly, I wouldn't get cancer. *You promised!*

—But you promised that children outlive their parents, that the old die first. *You owe me!*

—But you promised that marriage was forever.

—But you promised. . . .

You promised. What is God calling you to release from your tight grip? What are the debts you need to "dis-remember"—to forgive? We all have a list. I had one.

Like many of you, I've gone through surgery. What an ordeal! Yet even after the bright prognosis and a clean bill of health, I felt a great sense of "But you promised": My body should have worked. My arm, my liver, my kidney, my uterus—it should have worked, according to the medical journals and books. And if not, why couldn't I go to a doctor and get it fixed? To remove it was so final. Now it will never work because it's gone. Anger. Guilt. Blame. Sadness. And, finally, goodbye. What a long journey it was from a tight-fisted grudge match to an open hand! What an arduous journey it was from the former things to the new thing!

God indeed created something new. I've developed greater appreciation for these bones, this skin, this muscle, this chamber that I now have. I've found that I can even soar to new heights. For one thing, my body is lighter! I have surrendered the excess baggage of weight.

The newness that is within our reach is typically expressed by a twelve-year-old girl in Marilyn Ferguson's *Aquarian Conspiracy*. She says flying would be enjoyable if everyone could do it; otherwise, it would be conspicuous. She's right. Flying is conspicuous. But it is also contagious. So fly away. You will attract so much attention that people will ask you where you got your wings, where your source of strength is, how you lost your fear. And you can witness to the power in letting go, trusting God, and watching for something new. God will also supply you with journey mates who can also fly (so you won't be conspicuous).

> O freedom, O freedom. O freedom over me.
> And before I'd be a slave
> I'd be buried in my grave;
> And go home to my Lord and be free.

God Has a Master Plan For Your Life

A Plan for Good, Not Evil; for Peace, Hope, and Joy, Not Despair!

Peggy R. Scott

"For I know the thoughts that I think toward you, saith the LORD, thoughts of peace, and not of evil, to give you an expected end" (Jeremiah 29:11).

In the Revised Standard Version, the verse says, "For I know the plans I have for you, says the LORD, plans for welfare [well-being] and not for evil, to give you a future and a hope."

This message today is not a popular one; it is not usually discussed from the pulpit, but rather in family-group or individual counseling sessions. Yet, it is a subject that needs to be addressed in the churches.

It is directed toward two primary groups:

Rev. Peggy R. Scott is an ordained minister and evangelist and has worked in prison ministry, community development, and teaching. She was community development analyst for O.I.C. in Philadelphia before relocating to Southern California, where she served as director of Living Word School of Ministry in what was then known as Walnut Faith Center, Pomona, California.

Group #1: Adopted/foster children, stepchildren, children of divorced and/or unwed parents.

Group #2: All the mothers and fathers of these children and every potential parent.

Many of us can relate to these groups because someone we know, a family member, or we ourselves belong to one or both of them.

Oftentimes in the Black community we have been so concerned with daily survival that we have neglected to address how our behavior will affect our children.

This message is not intended to blame the parents for their decisions but is meant to offer support to the children, who are affected by adult decisions.

It is time for the church to respond to these situations, seeing them not as clinical or therapeutic problems, but as spiritual ones. (It may be necessary though, in some instances to view domestic situations clinically or therapeutically.) Some children adjust to these situations with little or no difficulty; others need special attention.

Let's examine what the Bible has to say about some children who were not reared by their natural parents and how God achieved a master plan for their lives.

In the book of Exodus, we find Moses, whose name means "drawn out" (because he was drawn out of the river). We are familiar with the story: how Pharaoh issued an order to kill at birth all the Hebrew male children in an attempt to decrease the population of Israel. Moses' mother, in defiance of Pharaoh's order and because of love for her child, placed Moses into a basket on the river. Ironically (but within God's plan for Moses' life), Pharaoh's daughter found Moses there and afterwards reared him as her son.

Moses, a member of the tribe of Levi, was born into slavery, the son of Amram and Jochebed and the brother of Aaron and Miriam. He was reared and educated, not by his natural parents, but by the daughter of the pharaoh. Moses was, therefore, of the household of the very king of Egypt who had kept the children of Israel in bondage. Moses was chosen by God to deliver his people out of bondage. God had a master plan for his life.

Let's examine the life of another child, Samuel. In First Samuel, we find that Samuel, whose name means "asked of God," was also not reared by his parents. Prior to his birth, Hannah, Samuel's mother, was barren. She prayed diligently to the Lord for a child, even making a vow to return the child to the Lord. Eli, the priest in the temple, revealed to Hannah that the God of Israel would grant her petition. When God did, Hannah kept her promise; after weaning Samuel, she gave him back to God. As a child, Samuel ministered unto the Lord in the temple. He became a prophet and judge of Israel, a devout man set apart for service to God. He had the responsibility of anointing the first and second kings of Israel, Saul and David. God had a master plan for his life.

God has a master plan for each of us—a plan for good, not evil; for peace, hope and joy, not despair.

Satan continually opposes our realizing God's plan for our lives. Satan has even convinced some people to believe that he does not exist; because of their intellect and environment they do not and will not acknowledge such a medieval concept as the devil.

However, there is biblical evidence to verify Satan's existence and motive. John 10:10 says that Satan, the thief, comes to steal, kill, and destroy. He comes to rob us of realizing that God has a specific purpose and plan for our lives. His plan is to prevent us from knowing God's plan.

How does Satan's plan operate, specifically in the cases mentioned in the beginning of my sermon? Satan plants seeds of discord in the minds of many children who are not reared by their natural parents or both partners. He takes advantage of these situations to sow seeds of resentment and feelings of rejection, guilt, disappointment, anger, pain, despair, and loneliness. Satan influences people to feel negative and then convinces them to conceal the feeling or to be angry.

All children are not affected by their families' dilemmas, but many children are deeply affected by family circumstances and experiences and require inner healing. They must be reassured periodically that no matter who their parents are or who did or did not rear them, God loves them and has a master plan for their lives. They must realize that although they were only procreated by their natural parents but not reared by them, God has said, "All souls belong to me" (Ezekiel 18:4).

Many of you today, both children and adults, have had these same feelings and experiences. Because of extenuating circumstances some adults have had to relinquish the responsibility of rearing their children to someone else. Some of you have done a good job of concealing your inner hurts; for many of you, your closest friends or relatives do not know how you feel.

Today I want you to know that Jesus knows exactly how you feel, not only because he is the Son of God and is omniscient—all-knowing—but because, as stated in Hebrews 4:15, "We have not an high priest which cannot be touched with the feeling of our infirmities. . . ." *The Amplified New Testament* says, "For we do not have a High Priest Who is unable to understand and sympathize and have a fellow feeling with our weaknesses and infirmities. . . ." Isaiah 53:4 says that Jesus bore our griefs and carried our sorrows.

Jesus, the Word, was made flesh and dwelt on earth. Seen from a natural plane, Jesus himself was a stepson and half brother. He was accepted and reared by Joseph, the carpenter. Spiritually, however, he was conceived by the Holy Spirit and is the Son of God.

God has a master plan for our lives. If we, children or adults, are to become effective Christians, we must receive an inner healing for all our hurts, pains, resentments, feelings of rejection, and other negative emotions. God wants to heal us; God cares about us. We can be healed today and begin to realize that God has a plan for us. But how can we be healed?

There are five steps in receiving inner healing: (1) *Believe and confess* — "If thou shalt confess with thy mouth the Lord Jesus, and shalt believe in thine heart that God hath raised him from the dead, thou shalt be saved" (Romans 10:9). (2) *Acknowledge that you are a new creature* — "Therefore, if any man be in Christ, he is a new creature: old things are passed away; behold, all things are become new" (2 Corinthians 5:17). (3) *Acknowledge that your name is in heaven* — ". . . but rather rejoice, because your names are written in heaven" (Luke 10:20). (4) *Acknowledge God as your true mother and father* — "When my father and mother forsake me, then the LORD will take me up [as his own]" (Psalm 27:10). (5) *Forgive* — ". . . forgive, and ye shall be forgiven. . . . Love ye your enemies, and do good, and lend, hoping for nothing again; and your reward shall be great, and ye shall be the children of the Highest" (Luke 6:37, 35).

Accept your family's circumstances; do not let them interfere with your relationship to God and with your spiritual growth. It is not so much what has happened to you as how you react to what has happened that matters.

If your situation is too painful, too much of a burden, too heavy a load to carry, then ask for forgiveness, and yield to Jesus. Allow the love of Jesus and the indwelling of the Holy Spirit to heal you today. "King Jesus will roll all burdens away."

Our Spiritual Account

Margrie Lewter-Simmons

Romans 14:11-12

April 15 is judgment time. The lines at post offices are from here to yonder. Millions of people all over America wait until the last minute to audit their accounts and report to Uncle Sam what has been happening for a whole year. Uncle Sam will make the final judgment on the taxes we have to pay on what we earned. Uncle Sam will check and double check! There will be many mistakes—many errors—many corrections! And after a while, "Sorry, but you owe us. . . ."

Paul was imagining such a figure or parable when he wrote to the people in the church at Rome, "So then every one of us shall give account of himself to God (Romans 14:12). The

Dr. Margrie Lewter-Simmons is pastor of the Assembly of Prayer Baptist Church in Roslyn Heights, Long Island, New York. She was a senior district manager for World Book, Inc., for twenty years before graduating from Adelphi University and then New York Theological Seminary. She earned the D.Min. at United Theological Seminary, Dayton, Ohio. Her parish is noted for moving from a store-front sanctuary to a building designed and built for them, with their own baptistry. In the New York area, this was a first for a female pastor.

Phillips version reads: "It is to God alone that we shall have to answer for our actions."

Let me hasten to say that I don't believe Paul was preaching "hellfire and damnation." In the early verses of Romans 14 Paul recorded disputes about who should eat what, who should fast, and a whole catalog of "ifs" and "buts," followed by condemnations of those who differed. Paul thought that the Roman believers were overly concerned about other people's books. He set the record straight: each of us is to focus meticulous care on his or her own books, "for we shall *all* stand before the judgment seat of Christ" (emphasis added).

Every one of us shall give account of ourselves to God! We read and hear of many people whose checking accounts in banks are overdrawn: people write bad checks, misappropriate funds, or even go to jail for some kind of fraud. Sometimes they even cheat on their taxes. But the day of reckoning (various auditing) will come, sure 'nuff!

We won't even mention our charge accounts at stores or our carefree spending—compulsive or otherwise. The trouble with money matters is that once we make a misfake with the figures, it's on the books somewhere; unless the whole mess is cleared up, everything after that will be all wrong. The balance will be off by the amount of the mistake. And sooner or later, we have to get it all straight! We have to audit the books.

Just as taxes come due, our spiritual audit is due. We are serious about other people's books; we wonder why God doesn't audit them sooner than it appears. But that's not our business. Suffice it to say that God *does* audit—and we'd better get our books straight, our spiritual accounts settled, right soon.

When we come, then, to the Lord's Supper, Paul's words to the church at Corinth have double significance: "Let every person examine the books—thoroughly careful of what is going down. Only then shall that person eat the bread and drink of the cup" (1 Corinthians 11:28, paraphrased).

Look at your accounts. What have we been petting and patting? What have we been sweeping under the rug? What have we been paying no attention to because it kinda hurts to look *with scrutiny*? As Paul said to the Romans, everyone, all of us, will have to give an account to God. We dare not come to the end with a whole lifetime to review from scratch. We would find too much involvement, too many altered specifications in varied periods to face at once. It is much better to set the record straight day by day; or when you come to church on Sunday; straighten it up week by week. And should some major problems arise in the ledger of life that take more time to clear up, for Christ's sake try to have them all straightened out once a month, for example, at Communion time.

If there are some errors in your lives like the errors in your check books, don't let the mistakes go on for a year (as may be done with taxes). You have to be careful because mistakes could all pile up to a *lifetime*'s worth of them. Now, I'm not talking about being mad at yourself, hating yourself, being guilt ridden, or running around nearly out of your mind because there are many sins that you *think* you have (and some of them may not even be sins). Being nervous, upset, and uptight about things you did and mistakes you made doesn't help *anything*! Some things you imagine to be problems just aren't there. And yet there are enough things that really *are* there for you to get busy rectifying since time is running out!

While we're at it, let's go over the books. Let's look at some methods of bookkeeping that might help with the audit of our lives. Look over your records. Turn your pages in the ledger of life back to a year ago. Have you hurt anybody?

One of the most dastardly things a person can do is to go through life hurting people's feelings. Life is much too short to be busy with wrong things. A spiritual person thinks about others, a spiritual person knows we're all God's children, created by God and responsible for spreading love whenever and wherever we can! When we draw ourselves up and push people around and hurt folks, we just can't possibly be ready for a spiritual audit.

As we continue to look at your books, we will inevitably

ask, "Lord, is it I? Have I loved everybody? Have I been consistent in my behavior?" If we were honest with ourselves, we'd admit that we do *hate*. That's a part of our spiritual account that we need to ask God's help to straighten out!

I'm sure you've never heard such a thing, but I have heard people say, "As long as I live, I'll never speak to that so-and-so again." Check your account! Ask the Lord to help you. Don't wait too long because too long can be *too late*. Straighten out your account. Correct your spiritual books before you get in big trouble. Old folks used to sing: "You better mind. Gotta give an account at the judgment. . . ."

Strangely enough, some of us live unto ourselves. In the Holy Book there's one concept that tells us we're supposed to see how much we did for somebody else. Jesus speaks to this particular concept in the parable of the last judgment. The folks said: "When did we not do good things in your name?" And the Lord of life will answer, "I don't even know you. As I look over the books, you don't even have an account registered. I can't find a record of your good deeds. When I was sick, I didn't hear from you. When there was a famine in the land and you had some food, you didn't give me any. I didn't have any clothes, and you turned me away. Did you give me a cup of cold water? No! It's not on the books anywhere. Get out! Depart! Exit!" Books are being kept on all of us and we had better get our spiritual accounts cleared up or adjusted before it is everlastingly too late. (The spiritual says, "He sees all you do; He hears all you say. My Lord's writin' all the time!")

Still another category in good bookkeeping is found in Matthew 5, where Jesus speaks of a selected audit. Blessed are the meek. Have you been meek or have you been running off at the mouth, bragging and offending people? Blessed are the peacemakers. Did you keep the peace or disturb the peace? Blessed are you when you shall be "'buked and scorned," reviled and persecuted, talked about and yet unwilling to fight back. These things happened for the Lord's sake. Blessed. Blessed—your books are in good shape.

One other means of adjusting your spiritual account can

be found in Paul's letter to the Galatians, chapter 5. There he talks about a special kind of bookkeeping called the "fruit system." If you go through the books and see what has been produced, then you get your account settled and straight with a good running balance. For the fruit of the spirit includes love, joy, peace, patience, goodness, gentleness, faith, meekness, temperance. Look over your books to see if you can find any love, any joy. Look over your books to see if you fly off the handle at the slighest provocation. Look over the pages to see where you've suffered long. Look over the pages to see where you've been gentle, good, faithful, meek, or temperate. Check your spiritual account via the fruit system.

One final concept is your *balance*, the previous balance. Peter said that if you come to the end of the record year and you have less than the previous year, you're in big trouble. "But grow in grace and in the knowledge of our Lord and Saviour Jesus Christ" (2 Peter 3:18). So, however good your balance sheet looks, if you haven't grown in grace, if you haven't grown in the joy of the Spirit, if you haven't grown in your capacity to forgive, if your faith cannot be measured as being deeper and more abiding than before, then you're in serious trouble. You're in deficit!

Peter's appearance of balance was misleading when he looked so good on the mountain of Transfiguration. You see, his earlier problem was still "swept under the rug" or hidden in a remote corner, so all the balances that followed were off because the previous balance included an error.

Peter found out about his previous balance on the night when our Lord came out of that horrible lynch trial and looked into Peter's eyes with knowing compassion. He reconciled the statement with repentance; the Good Book said, "He went out and wept bitterly."

When we come to partake of the Lord's Supper, we look at Jesus wounded for our transgressions, bruised for our iniquities, and yet willing to keep our accounts open until we get them balanced and in good order.

Let us all examine ourselves when we come to Communion

and pray that God will help us get our spiritual accounts ready for the audit, whenever it comes.

As Romans 14:11-12 reminds us: "For it is written, As I live, saith the Lord, every knee shall bow to me, and every tongue shall *confess* to God! So then every one of us shall give account of himself to God" (emphasis added).

God's Woman

Suzan D. Johnson Cook

"I also and my maidens will fast likewise; and so will I go in unto the king, which is not according to the law: and if I perish, I perish" (Esther 4:16).

Many preachers today wait until there is a special service for women, such as "Women's Day," before they'll preach a sermon about a woman of God. Unlike them, I like all the Scriptures all the time and find power in the word of God— in those stories about women *and* those about men, those about heroes and those about the defeated. Throughout the

Dr. Suzan D. Johnson Cook is founder and senior pastor of the Bronx Christian Fellowship in New York City. A graduate of Emerson College, Boston; Columbia University's Teachers College and Union Theological Seminary, New York City; and United Theological Seminary, Dayton, Ohio, she has served as a White House Fellow and a member of President Clinton's Initiative on Race. She is the only female chaplain for the New York City Police Department and the first woman elected officer of the Hampton Ministers' conference.

Scriptures we're able to see the mighty works of God, we're able to see God's limitless power. And so today, for just a little while, I'd like to focus attention on a mighty woman of God: Queen Esther.

Today's history books retell the stories told to many of us by our parents and grandparents about a scattered and an abused people—*our* people, Black people—who were brought to this strange land to live and work as slaves. We have had a disturbing history that is not very pleasant to remember or even speak about. It is the story of men and women, some of whom were once kings and queens in their homeland, who were freighted to this land like cattle, animals, or property. It is the sad story of a people dispersed through many different areas in an attempt totally to destroy their culture—*our* culture—and any reminder of who they—and we—were. But it is also the story of a people who, when at their lowest, found a Savior, a Liberator. How interesting—this painful yet joyful story of ours!

If you understand at all the depth of our African-American story, then you see that it would be a good background for this story of Queen Esther. For in her story we find that we were not the only people to be oppressed, and that as God delivered Esther and her people, God can and *will* deliver us if we only believe.

Esther was a Jewish woman living in Persia. She was in that land through the same circumstances that Black people came here: by enslavement. She was the second generation of those who had been enslaved, and so no one but an old cousin named Mordecai knew that she was a Jew. It was a secret, however. If the truth had been known, they would have been killed.

Have you ever felt that you had to hide your identity? Have you not been able to let yourself be known? I mean, you were not able to let folks know who you really were and what you really believed because you knew that there would be a great risk involved? It's hard when you want to be honest and truthful with folks and let them know all about you, but you really can't. It's terrible when you're in the midst of a multitude of people and can't find anyone around who's like you to whom you can talk. Many people go to church trying to find the "right" church where they can let things out. It's sad when even in the church of God, you feel all by yourself. Oh, it's a terrible feeling.

If you have felt this way, you can identify with Esther's predicament. Being a Jew and living in a Persian empire didn't really mix well, like oil and water. But Esther had to deal with life as it was presented to her, just as we must. The psalmist even spoke about this predicament when he wrote, "How shall we sing the LORD's song in a strange land?" We see that we are not the first to face displacement or to question why it happened to us.

Esther had no real support system with which to identify. She had no mother to "reach out and touch" and no sisters or brothers that she knew of; she had no one but her old cousin, Mordecai. This cousin helped to support her and take care of her. He worked in the king's court. He didn't have a big job; he was just a little civil servant who had to work each and every day to help make ends meet, just as you and I must do. But Mordecai loved his people and wanted the future generations to live in freedom and have a better life than he had had, just as many of us hope and pray that life will be easier for our children. I remember well how my parents had to work two and sometimes three jobs to help make ends meet. I would always ask them, "Why do you work so hard?" The answer would always be the same: "So that you can have it better than we've had it."

Now, in our story the Persian king was looking for a new wife to replace Queen Vashti, whom he had cut loose because she refused to dance nude in front of him and his friends. So he sent a search team to look throughout all the land for a new queen. I imagine that as all the women gathered, the scene was something like the Miss America pageant that we see today—the most "beautiful" women on parade. And of all the women that the king saw, the one he chose as his new wife was Esther, this Jew who was living in Persia. But, the king did not know that she was a Jew. She still could not let out the truth. (You know how we can keep things quiet that we don't want known.) All went well for a while. Then came a huge challenge for Esther, a chance to help her people. For the first time she was in a position to save someone else. Luke reminds us that "to whom much is given, of him will much be required" (Luke 12:48, RSV).

To fill you in on a few details of the story: Cousin Mordecai had refused to bow down to one of the king's princes, Haman. As a result, Haman arranged for a decree to be passed for all the Jewish people to be killed. Mordecai, knowing the situation, pleaded with Esther to save the Jewish people. He knew that Esther now had some influence with the king, for she was the queen. You know how some of us can get when we know people with power, or people we think have power. Usually, for selfish reasons, we begin to ask them to pull strings for us. But Mordecai knew that he was asking for help on behalf of a whole race of people. So he went straight to his cousin Esther—not to the chairman of the deacon board, not to his congressional representative, but straight to the source of salvation. He knew that if his people were going to survive, someone would have to intercede. Queen Esther would have to step in to halt a threat for which someone else was responsible.

Esther's story reminds me of some of us Black women and men who are trying to get it together, who want to do right. Yet our very existence is threatened for something completely beyond our control. We've been so scattered and dispersed for much of our lives that sometimes we feel that we have to disguise who we are and live a schizophrenic existence. It seems we can't tell folks who we really are. Many of us have an "identity crisis" and feel we can't tell people we're Black. We will go out of the way to tell them that we have every other kind of blood but Black blood. It's a sad story.

We can use many disguises. In the fifties women tried to disguise their blackness by using bleaching creams; in the sixties many tried to disguise their income levels by moving to the suburbs because they were embarrassed to say that they were poor. And now it's the eighties and folks are still trying to hide things.

Many of us feel that we can't even tell folks that we're Christian. Even right in God's house many of us are holding back. We hold back the Spirit when the Spirit comes. We don't want folks to know that we feel good and love the Lord. We can be so *cool* on God sometimes. We act cool when we don't say, "Amen," and know that the feeling has hit us, or when we don't shout even though the Spirit says to shout. And if we're out with non-Christian friends, many of us feel that we can't say a good word for the Lord and let them know that there's "something within me that holdeth the reign; something within me that I cannot explain." Disguises . . . because there's always a risk involved when you reveal who you are. And many of us, like Esther, do not find many people around to support us: no friends and few family members. We often feel all alone.

But God, being who he is, always places someone around us who will remind us of who we are, just as Mordecai reminded Esther of who she was. There's always someone around whom God will touch to reveal the responsibility that's attached to a position, whether it's that of a queen, or a deacon, or an usher. God is all-knowing and all-wise and so often touches the hand of a writer, like Paul, or the lips and heart of a preacher, like Martin Luther King, Jr., or the voice of a singer, like Mahalia Jackson bringing a message to us—a message not only of liberation but also of hope and of love.

So in the midst of this crisis in Persia, God spoke through a man—Mordecai—to remind a woman—Esther—that she was God's woman. And Esther realized that even though she was in a powerful position (in secular terms), she didn't have the real power that she needed. To be God's woman meant that she had to have a personal relationship with God. She had to get the power before she could go in to see the king. It's impossible to do things when you have the wrong kind of power. You can't use gas in an electric stove—it's the wrong kind of power.

But the joy came when Esther realized that she didn't need

to do a whole lot of talking about getting this power; she didn't need to run to people to ask them their opinion. Once she realized that she needed the right kind of power, she went to the Source. She sought the right kind of power for herself, the kind of power she would need if she was going to be any help to her people or herself. And to go to God, she could take off all the masks and disguises that were hiding who she really was. She could be real with God, for there was no one else she could talk with as openly and honestly.

Esther sought power through fasting and through prayer. Prayer is good and it is powerful. It opens the door for God to come into our lives and work. Prayer takes our humanity and lets us make contact with divinity. There's power in prayer. It brings us closer to God.

I enjoy praying, for I realize that it's a source of my strength. But every now and then I also realize that I need to fast, just as Esther had to fast. Fasting means to abstain from physical food so that one can be strengthened with spiritual food. It allows the impure to go out so that the pure can come in: pure love, pure joy, pure hope, pure peace. For through prayer and fasting we can have perfect peace and keep our minds stayed on God (see Isaiah 26:3). There are no hidden dangers, toils, or snares when one fasts and prays to God.

For Esther the real power came when she invited others to join with her in fasting and prayer. This meant that not only would she get power but also others would get power. It meant that others trusted her enough to join with her, for they needed power too. When you unveil yourself and take off all the disguises so that you can be God's woman (or God's man), then you become a mirror for others so that they can also see the glory of God. Somebody wrote a song with the lyrics "Walk together, children, and don't you get weary." We can't run this race all by ourselves. We need others to walk and run with us.

I look forward with great anticipation to prayer meetings and Bible study on Wednesday nights at our church because I realize that none of us can keep the faith alone, but together we can lift one another up and then we can lift up the name of Jesus. When I begin to get weak, there is someone there who can lift me up, and when I am strong, I can help someone else. That's part of the process of my becoming God's woman. When we share the power, then the power grows in each of us.

Even Jesus, the Son of the living God, who came into this world as God in the flesh, had to be hidden for a little while because King Herod would have killed him if he had found him. Yet, in God's time Jesus was able to reveal who he really was—the Messiah—for the prophecy of his coming had been fulfilled. When God speaks, when God touches us, we can take off all of the disguises, for we know, as the hymn says, that it is well with our souls.

Even Jesus, God's Son, had to fast and pray for a closer walk with God. When times became too hard for him to bear alone, he would go into the garden or to a mountaintop and have a talk with God. When we remove ourselves from the physical, the carnal, then we grow stronger in the spiritual.

So Queen Esther, this woman of God, fasted. Esther prayed. And when she came forth, she knew that she had a *holy boldness*. She knew that she would not have to fight alone; she would have God to fight for her.

Jesus fasted and Jesus prayed. He prayed for us even when we could not pray for ourselves. But he also invited others to join with him in prayer so that they could draw closer to God. Jesus had a *holy boldness*. Yet Jesus perished, not because of anything that he had done, but because of what humanity had done. There at Calvary—oh, I can see it now—while his mother and followers watched, he perished. And because he perished for us, we should not perish if we believe on him. John 3:16 tells us "God so loved the world that he gave his only begotten Son, that whosoever believeth in him should not perish, but have everlasting life." On Calvary, he perished. As they pierced his side, he perished. As the blood came running down, he perished. Now you and I have the gift of God if only we believe.

Esther found a personal relationship with God, but she couldn't include Jesus Christ in her testimony, for he had not yet been born. You and I, though, can rejoice today because we have a story to tell. It's a story about Jesus and his love. It's a story about the Savior who came into our lives and healed us, liberated us, and saved us. You and I should be able to step out with the boldness that Jesus had and tell the world that the Savior has come. When we feel that our burdens are heavy or that the weight of our entire race or the entire world is upon us, remember the mighty woman of God, Esther, who took the weight to the Lord. But also remember a man who was the mighty man of God, Jesus the Christ, who has empowered us to go forth into the whole world telling the good news. Yes, our history has pain in it, yet our lives today can have everlasting joy. It's a joy that the world doesn't give to you. It's a joy that history can't take from you. It's a joy that no one can take away.

Who is God's woman? The woman who knows God for herself, who has a personal relationship with Jesus the Christ. Who is God's woman? One who takes off the disguises, owns all the things that have been hidden, and opens up to God. This is God's woman, the woman who gives her life to Jesus Christ. Amen.

Additional Sermons Published by Judson Press

Best Black Sermons, William Philpot, ed. 1972. Sermons that emphasize black dignity and proclaim God's power. 0-8170-0533-1

From Mess to Miracle and Other Sermons, William D. Watley. 1989. 0-8170-1154-4

Outstanding Black Sermons, J. Alfred Smith, ed. 1976. 0-8170-0664-8

Outstanding Black Sermons, Volume 2, Walter B. Hoard, ed. 1979. 0-8170-0832-2

Outstanding Black Sermons, Volume 3, Milton Owens, Jr., ed. 1982. 0-8170-0973-6

Preaching in Two Voices, William D. Watley and Suzan D. Johnson Cook. 1992. 0-8170-1173-0

Sermons from the Black Pulpit, Samuel D. Proctor and William D. Watley. 1984. Thirteen sermons that call for a renewed commitment to discipleship. 0-8170-1034-3

Sermons on Special Days—Preaching Through the Year in the Black Church, William D. Watley. 1987. Sixteen sermons for all celebrations of the Christian year. 0-8170-1089-0

Those Preaching Women, Volume 2, Ella Pearson Mitchell, ed. 1988. 0-8170-1131-5

Women: To Preach or Not to Preach? 21 Outstanding Black Preachers Say Yes! Ella Pearson Mitchell, ed. 1991. 0-8170-1169-2

PThose Preachin' Women

WITHDRAWN

DATE DUE